THE
LAST
SAFE
INVESTMENT

THE
LAST
SAFE
INVESTMENT

SPENDING NOW TO INCREASE YOUR TRUE WEALTH FOREVER

BRYAN FRANKLIN AND
MICHAEL ELLSBERG

PORTFOLIO / PENGUIN

PORTFOLIO / PENGUIN

An imprint of Penguin Random House LLC
375 Hudson Street
New York, New York 10014
penguin.com

ISBN 978-1-59184-611-6

Printed in the United States of America
1   3   5   7   9   10   8   6   4   2

Set in Garth Graphic
Designed by Sabrina Bowers

BRYAN'S DEDICATION:

For Jennifer Russell
The lover who created me, my true companion,
my wife, my one

MICHAEL'S DEDICATION:

For my coauthor Bryan
My great mentor in business and life

CONTENTS

THE
LAST
SAFE
INVESTMENT

INTRODUCTION

"**I**sn't this the part where you give me your advice for what I should do with my life?" Stephen (not his real name), eighteen years old, dressed up in cap and gown, wanted to give his father a chance. In many ways, at least symbolically, a *last chance*. Graduation day, he thought, is the time when a typical father gives a typical son "the speech." Imparting the wisdom the father (or mother) has gained through decades of life experience to help shortcut the son's (or daughter's) path toward success. So the children can learn as many lessons the easy way and as few the hard way as possible.

But Rick (also not his real name) was short on advice.

He opened his mouth to speak but words didn't come out. Rick reached for what he could tell his son to do, but all that came up were his past mistakes. He paused, wishing badly that Stephen could somehow learn to avoid them.

MISTAKE 1: He leveraged the house with too much debt and ended up underwater.

MISTAKE 2: He spent too much money on things with motors (cars, boats, Jet Skis, motorcycles) and other luxury stuff that was supposed to make him happy but didn't end up doing so. Now Rick wishes he had the money instead.

MISTAKE 3: He went into business by himself but didn't learn how to get customers, relying on a trickle of word-of-mouth referrals to put food on the table. Lean times were really lean and really tense. Fat times could pay the bills and give him extra cash (which usually got spent on luxury stuff—see Mistake 2).

MISTAKE 4: He never found work he could do happily in older age. With no ability to retire anytime soon, at fifty-two years old, he dislikes his work, and therefore, dislikes much of his life, looking forward only to the short respites he gets from work to spend time with his son and other loved ones.

MISTAKE 5: He invested in stocks he didn't understand. Lost those investments.

MISTAKE 6: He spent savings on remodeling the house, betting on the housing market to give him a big payback. That didn't work out. Much of his savings went literally down the drain in his bathroom and kitchen remodels.

Rick looked at his son Stephen. Tall. Put-together. Even-keeled. He got immaculate grades. When Rick put Stephen on his work crews, his son was usually the hardest and most dependable worker. Rick was silent for a moment more, gagging on feelings of inadequacy.

During his father's silence, Stephen had mixed feelings. He loved his dad and appreciated him. But he also felt kind of let down. If each generation is supposed to reach further up the ladder than the last, why was he being handed a ladder with all the rungs sawed off?

"Look, Stephen, you're going to be graduating in a few hours. I'd love to be able to tell you what to do to be successful in life. To make sure you don't end up where I am. But honestly I think you'd do a better job figuring it out for yourself. All I've got is bad advice and sad stories."

A version of this same conversation could be happening in thousands of families (perhaps millions) every graduation season. Eighteen- to twenty-two-year-olds look up to their parents for one last set of instructions before leaving the nest, but because of the decline of America's middle class, and the near-total annihilation of the lower class, parents just don't have a map of the new territory.

The future-planning impulse is to tell the children to *invest*. But in what? With the most recent financial crisis, subprime housing implosions, and real estate bubbles popping, where are the safe investments?

This book is dedicated to the multitude of Stephens and the multitude of Ricks, regardless of your age, stage of life, marital status, or financial situation: we believe in you. In this book, we deliver to you what we believe is the best advice ever assembled on the topic of how to invest for a successful life for yourself, financial and otherwise, in this new postcrisis landscape.

No matter how many decades have passed between you and your formal education, we also encourage you to think of today as graduation day *for you*.

Use this manual to start making better life choices that can lead not only to a more financially secure future, but can relieve your stress about money and retirement and also make yourself truly happy in the process.

ALL FACD UP

Here's the "bait" part of the usual financial bait and switch:

You too can be rich! All you have to do is follow this advice. Work hard and save as much money as you can. Don't drink premium coffee, and be sure to watch movies at home on date night instead of going to a movie theater. You'd be crazy to spend any money at all now because, if you look at the long-term average of stocks, they compound at 7 percent a year above inflation. *Don't you know about the magic of compounding returns?* If you just sock that saved money away now in a low-fee index fund, a minuscule amount now will be worth *millions* by the time you're ready to retire. In fact, due to the miracle of compounding returns, that latte you just bought could buy you a *trip to Hawaii* during your retirement years! So start young, live frugally now, and watch your wealth rise over the long haul. The only other thing that is acceptable to spend money on, aside from higher education (which we all know guarantees you easy access to a good job for reasonable tuition fees), is a home. Home values compound just as stocks compound, and they never go down. In fact, you can ride your rising, compounding 401(k) and home equity right into a wealthy retirement.

We call this Financial Advice Commonly Delivered, or FACD for short.

People who were FACD over the last one and a half decades don't tend to be too happy these days. Over the last fifteen years, the S&P 500 has risen at an annualized rate of about 1.9 percent above inflation per year, and home values have barely beaten inflation.[1] These are not anywhere near the kinds of returns one can hope to build a "nest egg" on via capital appreciation. People who were hoping to retire on their financial and real estate investments over the last two decades generally feel burned out, spent—perhaps even used—by the financial program they were supposed to follow, and by the financial advisers, money managers, stockbrokers, retirement planners, and personal finance "gurus" who sold them on this program. Whether you think these role players maliciously misled us for their own gain or were merely swept up in a mass cultural delusion, it's clear the FACD plan has failed to deliver on its promises over the last fifteen years.

For a variety of reasons, it has become very hard for the

average investor to grow significant wealth on the financial and housing markets, no matter how much is scrimped and saved. That is the "switch" part of the usual financial bait and switch.

Millions of Americans are disillusioned with the traditional model for investing to secure a prosperous future. That model has failed them bitterly over the last twenty years, and they are looking for an alternative.

This book presents that alternative.

THE AMERICAN DREAM REQUIRES YOU TO BE ASLEEP

Here are the two main ways most people in the middle class have tried (and usually failed) to build wealth and get ahead: first, borrowing great sums for higher education, in the hope that better academic credentials and academic skills will lead to a higher income; and second, scrimping and saving, investing that money in retirement funds and mortgaged real estate in the hope that small amounts of capital will grow into larger amounts later, and that one day they can stop working entirely and live on that money.

Our beef with the first method was presented exhaustively in Michael's book *The Education of Millionaires* (which featured Bryan's story as the opener to the book). To recap here: trying to build financial security by borrowing large amounts of money in the pursuit of higher academic credentials has been an unqualified disaster for millions of young Americans, particularly those graduating in the last decade.

Student debt in the United States has surpassed the amount of outstanding credit card debt in the nation, surging past the $1 trillion mark. All the students who were obedient to their parents' and teachers' shepherding in the last decade are now finding that they were actually being shepherded into a debt slaughterhouse. The Federal Reserve Bank of New York recently announced that, of all student loans in the repayment phase (after students have graduated), *30 percent* are delinquent by ninety days or more on their balances, including a total of 21 percent in full-on default.[2] Yes, it's true. Close to one-third of student debt holders, once they are out of school, are now delinquent on their student loans. The relatively recent cultural experiment of sending millions of kids to college on high amounts of borrowed money is turning out to be a disaster of housing-crash proportions. "The crisis . . . is about to break," writes Joseph Stiglitz, Nobel Prize–winning former chief economist for the World Bank, in a *New York Times* blog post analyzing the data. The piece was titled "Student Debt and the Crushing of the American Dream."[3]

The second strategy middle-class people have been told to follow to build wealth and get ahead in life is the FACD plan. To recap, here are the basic steps of that plan:

1. Earn money from working.
2. Save as much of that money as possible, delaying gratification.
3. Invest savings in things outside of your control (stocks, bonds, real estate).
4. Reinvest earnings from investments over several decades.
5. Retire from working, and start spending your investment capital.
6. Be happy, via the gratification delayed from step 2.

Graphically, this plan looks something like this:

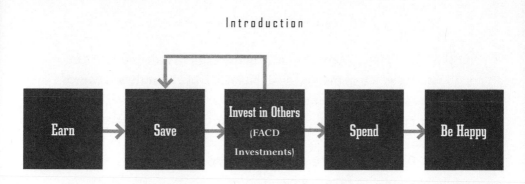

While there is nothing inherently wrong with any of these steps individually, when taken together, and in this order, they constitute a plan that is totally unworkable.

Most people—even those who are near the top of the pack in terms of earning power—fail to save a significant portion of their earnings. Most people who invest in the stock market or real estate fail to meet their financial goals through those investments (the average person is more likely to lose money than gain over the long term when adjusted for inflation). Most people are unable to successfully delay gratification and end up spending too much too early to stick to the plan. And even for the very few who are able to follow this plan successfully, they are not necessarily able to make themselves happy just because they are no longer required to work, scrimp, and save just to get by. Free time alone cannot make you happy. Any plan that doesn't work for most of the people who follow it is simply a *bad plan.* It's not just that it's warm in here, you're actually in the frying pan. You're in the frying pan because you've been *taught* that there's a fire out there that's even hotter.

We can show you where there's no fire, so you can jump—safely.

CRITERIA FOR A WORKABLE PLAN

For a personal financial planning model to be truly credible, it can't merely do a better job of delivering on the countless broken promises of the FACD plan. A proposed alternative plan that does a *better* but still *insufficient* job of meeting your financial and nonfinancial needs won't cut it. For any proposal to rise to the level of *credible*, it must not only be better, but fully satisfy each of the following criteria:

1. It must work for people who have little or no money to invest now.
2. It must not rely on uncommon skills or extraordinary intelligence.
3. It must not rely on willpower, or behaviors that people know they *should* do but few actually do.
4. It must not rely on deprivation, long periods of postponing happiness, or significantly lowering your standard of living.
5. It must not be a closed, zero-sum system that necessitates *losers* in order to have *winners*. (In any game where there are winners and losers, relying on continually being one of the lucky few winners isn't viable in the long run.)
6. It must increase (rather than decrease) in viability as more people adopt it, with the capability of scaling to 100 percent of the population without breaking.
7. It must succeed in an environment of ever-increasing uncertainty and ever-decreasing stability in the job and financial markets.
8. It must not rely on extracting more value from the system than is put in.
9. It must take into account the accelerated increases in average life span, including the possibility of unforeseen radical improvements in human life expectancy.
10. It must be completely initiated and maintained by you, rather than depending on the performance of

companies, agencies, lawmakers, home prices,
stock indices, or other factors beyond your control.

These criteria may seem impossibly restrictive, but read the list again, and consider the implications of any plan that fails to meet one or more of these: at best, it might work for some of the people some of the time, which is like suggesting you gamble with your life savings and your future.

Throughout this book, we invite you to measure our proposed alternative plan against all of these criteria, and determine for yourself if you're holding in your hands the roadmap to the wealth you desire in all areas of your life.

Though all the criteria are important, the most significant to us is the last one: it must depend on you. This works to reduce the gambling element as much as possible, by precluding investment in things outside of your own control, or your own ability to predict. The safest investment is the thing you have the most control over: yourself. The conventional wisdom is that you should leave your financial life up to the experts, giving up control in exchange for promises of wealth and security. However, the experts have proven that they are unable to deliver on these promises.

If you remove from consideration all the investments that are completely untested (such as brand-new crypto-currencies), or that involve negative gains when accounting for inflation (such as most "safe" bonds), or that involve unpredictable periods of catastrophic results for the average investor (such as the stock market and real estate market), by process of elimination you're left with yourself as the one remaining safe investment.

We have asked thousands of people what they want from their careers and financial lives. We always hear some version of the same three answers: happiness, freedom, and financial security (also sometimes described as "safety"). Because you can't sustain happiness or freedom without safety, we view safety as the most fundamental of the three. Our model optimizes for both your financial safety and your ability to experience that safety subjectively (i.e., to "feel safe"), which we believe are the most important deliverables of any financial plan.

To achieve this, a financial plan must take into account your whole financial ecosystem, not just the number at the end of your balance sheet. Financial wealth only represents one-quarter of your financial ecosystem, and therefore is unable to provide what we call *True Wealth*. Money alone cannot make you happy, cannot make you free, cannot make you feel safe, cannot make you feel powerful, cannot make you creatively expressed, cannot make you feel loved, and therefore cannot make you truly wealthy.

To be truly wealthy, you must also be able to convert that money into the kinds of life experiences you most enjoy. You must also be able to learn and grow from those experiences so they enrich who you are rather than just being consumed as passing entertainment. In essence, you must be able to convert life experience into self-development. You must also be able to convert the ways that you've been enriched and developed into new abilities to serve and create value for others, and lastly you must learn how to convert the ability to be more valuable to others into more money.

This is your entire financial ecosystem, and if you are able to have as much access as you want to each of these four areas, then you will have True Wealth.

FINANCIAL ECOSYSTEM: PATH TO TRUE WEALTH

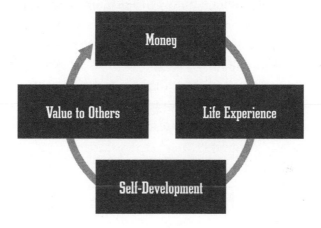

The FACD plan doesn't work because it only operates on one aspect of the whole financial ecosystem, often at the expense of the other aspects. These other aspects are essential to our ability to *experience* financial safety, enjoyment, and freedom, but are often disregarded as nonfinancial because they are not physical or tangible. But the nonphysical, nontangible aspects of our financial life are incredibly important to us, and they are an inseparable component of your financial ecosystem.

We do not tolerate them being disregarded, which is one reason the FACD plan fails.

THE SELF-AMPLIFYING FINANCIAL ECOSYSTEM

The alternative to the FACD plan is the SAFE plan, which stands for Self-Amplifying Financial Ecosystem.

Rather than relying on a single point of failure, such as the rate of asset growth in your portfolio, the SAFE plan outlines how to set up a *system* of interconnected parts that all work together to reliably produce financial and nonfinancial rewards.

The SAFE plan helps you change the way you look at your career, your spending habits, your use of free time, your friends, and your financial situation to get them to work together, each amplifying the impact of the others, in much the same way that a strong team amplifies the impact of each individual.

Here is a graphic representation of the plan:

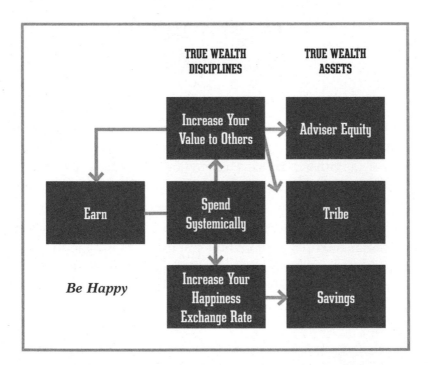

As you can see from the graphic above, the SAFE plan calls for developing three disciplines (Spend Systemically, Increase Your Value to Others, and Increase Your Happiness Exchange Rate), which lead to developing three assets (Adviser Equity, Tribe, and Savings). We'll be describing these "True Wealth disciplines" and "True Wealth assets" in detail throughout the rest of this introduction and offering approaches for investing in them in the chapters that follow.

THE 1ST TRUE WEALTH DISCIPLINE:
Spend Systemically

Both the traditional FACD plan and our new SAFE plan discussed here use your current level of earning as the given input. However, the first transition in the SAFE plan is from earning straight to spending, which from a willpower point of view is a lot more probable, not to mention more delightful, than going from earning to "save as much money as possible." But in order for spending money to lead to your True Wealth, you must understand Systemic Spending—the first of three True Wealth disciplines.

If you are like most people, when you make a decision about how to spend your time, money, or attention, you evaluate the options in a compartmentalized manner. That is, you evaluate the decision based on whether that spending will improve just one context of your life, what we will call its "original context." For example, if you are contemplating purchasing a new TV, you might evaluate whether the TV will improve your experience within its original context of "electronics for entertainment." If you are contemplating spending on a trip to Hawaii, you might evaluate whether that expenditure will improve your experience within its original context of "vacation." And so forth.

In this book, we advocate a simple mind-set shift. We call it Systemic Spending. To shift to Systemic Spending, think about your life as a system of interconnected parts. Any systems engineer will tell you that local optimization—or improving a part of the system based on a narrow set of criteria that does not take into account the rest of the system—will always degrade the system's performance over time. If taken far enough, local optimization will eventually drive any system to a fatal breaking point—which is a pretty fair description of the state of the global economy and the economic outlook for all but the most advantaged people alive today.

Most people tend to view any particular expenditure of time, money, or attention only in terms of how it affects its original context. They view exercise, for example, in terms of how well it flattens their tummy or bulks up their muscles. They view their jobs and investments primarily in terms of how much money they provide. They view their relationships purely in terms of the enjoyment they get from spending time with another person. This is exactly the form of local optimization that breaks down overall system performance—in this case the system of your life.

In Systemic Spending, you evaluate how any particular piece of spending improves *every other* context in your life, *aside from* its original context. This is how to become a systems engineer for your own life, lifestyle, and livelihood. Broadly speaking, there are six major contexts most people care about in their lives.

SYSTEMIC SPENDING CHART

Consider any purchase, large or small. Write it down in the Purchase column next to its corresponding category. How does that purchase improve or harm the other areas of your life?

	PURCHASE	IMPACT
HEALTH		
Nutrition		
Fitness		
Sleep		
RELATIONSHIPS		
Sex		
Love/Romance		
Community of Friends & Family		
MONEY		
Income		
Net Worth		
Career		
CULTURE		
Art/Entertainment		
Travel/Leisure		
Home/Environment		
PURPOSE		
Legacy		
Contribution to Others		
Spirituality		
CAPABILITY TO PROVIDE VALUE		
Creativity		
Influence		
Knowledge		

Systemic Spending involves looking at your spending in *every* context in your life, in terms of how it amplifies or reduces the benefits in the *other* contexts. How does this new way of spending change things? It has the potential to transform everyday consumption into *investing.*

How does it work? Here is a simple example. Imagine you and someone named John each have enough money to spend an evening at the movies with some friends. John calls his buddies from work and they decide to take in the latest action flick. With a large popcorn, candy, soda, and movie tickets for him and his friends, John spends $60.

You look at the available films, and you notice that there's a new documentary about an issue that has been in the news a lot lately. While the action film looks fun, you remember that one of your business mentors cares about that issue a great deal. You decide to get a small group of people together, including a woman you don't know as well but who is well connected in your industry. You invite them to join you for the movie and a discussion afterward to explore the topic of the film. You buy your ticket and a bottle of water for each of your friends, spending a total of $60.

Now, here's the question: between you and John, which one of you *consumed*, and which one of you *invested*? To a typical economist, financial planner, or money manager, the answer is obvious. Both you and John *consumed* with your $60. John bought entertainment, food, and a beverage. You bought entertainment and beverages. The economist might agree, personally, that your consumption was somehow more "wholesome" or "virtuous" than John's. But in the typical worldview of the economist, financial adviser, or personal finance guru, it was still consuming, not investing, because there was no expectation of future returns on food, beverages, or movies.

However, let's look at your choice of entertainment experiences systemically. Instead of evaluating your experience in terms of how much fun you had—the original context of Entertainment—how does this expenditure affect *other* contexts?

HEALTH. Not only is water more healthy than soda, the lack of caffeine will positively affect your ability to sleep and the amount of time you spend in REM, the most nourishing and vital part of your sleep cycle. The fact that you bought water for your guests will make them less likely to drink sodas with sugar, caffeine, or other chemicals and will better hydrate them, which is an important part of keeping spirits up during the conversation afterward that could include intense emotional sharing.

RELATIONSHIPS. An open dialogue among people you respect on an issue that they care about is potent as a formidable relationship builder. Your friendships with everyone present will deepen—far more than if you simply "spent time" together.

CAREER. Your caring and contribution to get involved with the passions and concerns of your business mentor will strengthen your relationship with him, and his respect and gratitude for you will make a memorable impression on the influential woman you are just getting to know. Your leadership of a high-quality group of people involved in a high-quality discussion will give you experience leading groups and taking on tough issues in professional contexts as well.

PURPOSE. An evening like the one you orchestrated will likely spur similar ideas among your friends in the future, and you will enjoy the satisfaction of contributing to the lives of others, which is at the core of the most satisfying answers to the question "What is my purpose in life?"

CAPABILITY TO PROVIDE VALUE. Even if the movie itself offers no meaningful insights, the discussion afterward is sure to expand your knowledge, your influence among your friends, and perhaps spur creativity about how to think about complex issues.

Every context other than the original context of Entertainment is positively affected by your choice. How much did John's junk food and action movie enhance his Health, Relationships, Wealth, Purpose, or Ability to Contribute? The contrast is striking.

If you're just going to a movie for its entertainment value, to get a few laughs or see things explode, that keeps entertainment within its original context. That's fine, but it's not investing. It's still consuming. However, when seen systemically, the same $60 starts to look like an investment, not an act of consumption. The essence of consumption is that something gets "used up," and in so doing loses value. The reason economists would say John's movie was consumption is that it got "used up" over its useful life of about ninety minutes. Your movie also got "used up," in the same ninety minutes, so economists would classify it as consumption as well. But the value of your movie experience, when viewed in a systemic context, is likely to last many years and go up over time, not down.

We've been taught that buying shares in an Internet company is investing and buying groceries is spending. Buying gold coins and stashing them in a safe is investing, while buying a gold watch and wearing it on your wrist is spending. Because the vast majority of readers don't have much money left over to invest after all their "spending," this belief leads to counting themselves out as investors. Why go to the trouble of learning how to be a wise investor if you have only a few thousand dollars each year to invest anyway? It's not as if you can save $100 per month and one day save up to buy a mansion and a yacht.

Consider what happens instead if you view *everything* you buy as an investment—as you must in order to adopt the habit of Systemic Spending. If you spend $65,000 per year after taxes on living and discretionary expenses, that means you are actually investing $65,000 per year. When you bought this book, you "invested" in a book. When you pay your rent you are "investing" in a month's stay in your apartment. While it's true that books and rent aren't likely to make you much money back *directly*, you can still measure their return in terms of their long-term benefits to you.

When you view spending this way, suddenly you realize that you have a lot more gas in the tank. Instead of investing a few thousand dollars per year, which is all that most Americans are typically able to save per year, now you are investing the sum of all your expenses, each year. That is a significantly larger pool of resources with which to invest each year. If you were going to invest nearly all your annual post-tax income, wouldn't you want to learn a little bit about how to make the best choice for your future?

With Systemic Spending, which we teach in this book, every time you spend money you have an opportunity to practice your investment thinking and leverage your spending to create the best possible future because the side effects of every purchase all add up to create the life you most want.

THE 2ND TRUE WEALTH DISCIPLINE:
Increase Your Value to Other People

Whereas the heart of the FACD plan is attempting to increase your financial net worth via increased portfolio value, the heart of the SAFE plan is the discipline of increasing your value to other people.

Some people are uncomfortable with the idea of "increasing your value to other people," as it seems to imply that some individuals are inherently more or less valuable. Others are uncomfortable with the idea because they want to be valued for who they are, and consider any efforts to change the perception of their value to be manipulative.

And yet, in any given context, you place a specific and distinct value on the behavior of other people. If you needed life-saving surgery, you would value an accomplished surgeon's work with a scalpel more than a first-year intern's, even as you held both people to have equal intrinsic value as humans. In general, you value behavior that is more skilled, trustworthy, caring, aesthetically pleasing, powerful, and credible. Even more, you value behavior that is in line with your present interests, objectives, and needs. The act of someone's giving you a canteen of water would be highly valued when you're stranded in a desert, and much less so while you're scuba diving.

Therefore "your value" to other people is not intrinsic to you at all. It is defined by the *match* between your behavior and other people's desired outcomes. Investing in your value to other people is really about investing in your ability to *detect* other people's desired outcomes and *demonstrate behavior* that is consistent with achieving those outcomes.

The immediate benefit of investing in your ability to be valuable to others is an increase in your earning potential. If you want to increase the output of any system, it's common sense to apply effort or resources to the highest leverage point— that is, the point in the system where the smallest incremental change creates the biggest change in output. Rather than focusing on traditional investments outside your control, we believe your earning potential, via an increased value to others, is that leverage point in your financial ecosystem.

Professional investors know that the best investments have

variability (their value can be low or high, allowing for opportunity to profit) and predictability (the causes of value fluctuation are foreseeable, to savvy investors at least). This allows a person who is paying attention to "buy low, sell high" with confidence. Without variability, an asset's value would stay the same in the future and couldn't offer any gains. And without some confidence that you can predict if it will go up or down, purchasing that asset is just gambling.

We suggest that your earning potential is the most variable and predictable asset on Earth. Consider the difference in earning potential between the CEO of any Fortune 1000 company and a beggar in the streets of Rajasthan. Can you think of another type of asset with as much variability? Not only is the outcome of this fluctuation in your future earning power highly variable, but the causes of variability are foreseeable and responsive to your input. Through investment in your professionalism, skills, relationships, network, and longevity, you have more control over future gains than with any other investment.

There are a nearly unlimited number of skills you can invest in that will increase your value to others in some way. While investing in random schemes to improve your earning potential will not likely secure your future wealth, this book is an investment guide that shows you exactly which self-investments are the most universally valued and therefore valuable. We focus on the *match* between your behavior and the needs, desires, incentives, and objectives of those around you. If you pay attention to that match, you can learn *how to know* which skills are worth real dollars and therefore worth investing in. The more you practice the discipline of being valuable to others, the better you'll get at learning how to invest in becoming more valuable to others, and the more opportunities to provide value you'll see. This also creates a self-amplifying effect, continually adding to your base earnings, which in turn gives you more resources to invest. We describe a roadmap for increasing your value to others, and a variety of ways to convert that value to earnings, in the chapters on Super Skills. Though increasing your value to others is the most reliable way to get more money in the future, its value is totally independent of money or any economic force, including the currency itself. No matter what uncertainty the future holds for the global economic climate, "being valuable to others" will never be obsolete, irrelevant, or valueless.

THE 3RD TRUE WEALTH DISCIPLINE:
Improve Your Happiness Exchange Rate

Your financial activities in life are aimed at creating results in both the external and internal realms. You want a certain amount of money in the bank, and a certain amount of material comfort (external rewards), but you also want those rewards to *feel* a certain way: that is, you want to *feel* happy, free, secure, etc. We call these twin aims *external wealth* and *internal wealth*.

Consider what would be missing if either the internal or the external wealth were not in place. Imagine if, perhaps through some philosophical or spiritual belief system, you managed to find a way to make yourself wildly happy and free (internal wealth), but you and your loved ones were struggling for lack of the basic necessities of life (external impoverishment). Or, imagine that you were a multimillionaire, but plagued by a persistent feeling that you had to earn even *more* money in order to be worthy of basic love. (If you've never spent time with multimillionaires, you might be surprised how common this kind of emotional situation is among them.) Both scenarios, while rich in one form of wealth, are impoverished overall for lack of True Wealth.

Your core drive to succeed financially—including the drive

that motivated you to pick up this book—depends on the idea that external wealth can be converted to internal wealth. Your credit card statement is a testimony to your repeated attempts at this conversion on a daily basis, with varying degrees of success.

Consider the purchase of a small ordinary consumable: a margarita. In most cases, it is not the least expensive, nor the most thirst quenching, nor the most salty, nor the most fruity, nor the most alcoholic drink available. It isn't optimized for being the *most* of any of its own qualities. So, for those millions of people who drink margaritas each day, why is this choice selected?

It's as if each person has an internal wealth finance department measuring the account balances in the various types of experiences we most want, and evaluating the likely debits and credits of every possible choice on each account. You might have an account for "social status" and one for "feeling attractive" and one for "the feeling of accomplishment" and one for "freedom" and one for "comfort" and one for "feeling lovable" and so on.

As you hold a drink menu in your hand, the internal wealth finance department in your head imagines purchasing the margarita, and if it can exchange external wealth for enough increases in the hundreds of different internal wealth account balances, you get a "green light" signal to buy the drink. For example, a $15 margarita might seem like a "better deal" than a $7 shot of tequila to your internal accountants, because of the increase in the "fun" or "feeling like I'm on vacation" or "time spent with others" account balances that you don't get with the other choice.

We call the measurement of this method of exchanging external wealth for internal wealth your "Happiness Exchange Rate." We call it this because when you add up all the balances from all the internal accounts, the sum total is a decent approximation of your general "happiness," which is what you are "exchanging" your external wealth for. As the term suggests, each person maintains a degree of efficiency when exchanging money for happiness, which varies wildly from person to person. This difference in Happiness Exchange Rate has a massive impact on your sense of financial success and financial security, because it determines how much money you need to spend in order to achieve the same level of happiness.

The problem is, as a species, we are laughably incompetent at predicting which purchases will actually have the intended effect on our internal balances. It's as if our internal wealth finance department is entirely staffed by drunk imbeciles. They have good intentions—to monitor our internal and external wealth and suggest beneficial exchanges—they're just going about it in a massively ineffective, inefficient way.

Imagine going through your bank statements for the last year and listing the *internal* wealth experience that you were hoping to gain from each purchase. If you scored each item based on the degree and duration you actually enjoyed that specific experience, you'd see that you rarely got what you were paying for. Did that dress make you feel as beautiful as you thought it would? Did that new luxury watch make you feel successful? How did your last meal feel an hour after you ate? While you may have enjoyed your purchase momentarily, it is just as likely that the underlying need that drove your purchasing decision remained unmet, or worse, was even intensified.

There is no area of human activity in which more money is wasted than in people's use of money in the attempt to obtain various forms of internal wealth. Very likely, *you* are hemorrhaging large amounts of money and time in the process of inefficiently trying to obtain internal wealth.

When viewed this way, your current Happiness Exchange Rate is likely your biggest expense, regardless of your bank balance. It consumes most of your current resources now, and unless you change, it is likely to consume most of anything you may have saved for retirement as well.

An efficient Happiness Exchange Rate is vital to your SAFE plan, regardless of whether you are materially rich or materially poor. Imagine two people in their retirement, who both have saved the same amount of money. But one has spent the last three decades learning how to convert external wealth into her own internal happiness, at the most efficient possible Happiness Exchange Rate. The other ignored his Happiness Exchange Rate and assumed that the amount of his external wealth was the only factor. Obviously the quality of the first person's life and therefore the success of her life plan is far superior, because she gets far more *internal* wealth for every unit of external wealth. The second person might as well be flushing most of his money down the toilet, accumulating a vast array of material objects, only some of which actually satisfy him. The first person is able to purchase only that which will work to systemically support her deepest desires, such as those for love, truth, belonging, and freedom.

Unlike traditional cost cutting, the exercise of eliminating tens or even hundreds of thousands of dollars of unnecessary personal expenses through improving your Happiness Exchange Rate is generally pleasurable. It involves developing the *skill* of being happy (yes, it is a skill), as well as paying close attention to the factors that contribute to your most (and least) rewarding experiences. It does *not* involve using willpower to resist spending time and money, or cutting out life's pleasures.

One definition of addiction is the inability to derive pleasure from more and more extreme experiences. And the ability to derive extreme pleasure from more and more mundane experiences might be described as enlightenment. Every time you make a purchase, your Happiness Exchange Rate places you somewhere on that continuum, and the SAFE plan calls for you to continuously evolve your ability to move toward the side of financial enlightenment.

FROM TRUE WEALTH DISCIPLINES COME TRUE WEALTH ASSETS

True Wealth allows you to continually and automatically generate the external circumstances that foster the deepest experiences you seek—longing for such things as love, truth, freedom, and safety—combined with the capacity to derive internal fulfillment from those experiences. True Wealth assets are all of the external things that work together to generate those circumstances on your behalf, including your web of human relationships, various forms of equity, and savings accounts.

For something to qualify as a True Wealth asset, it must continue to do its job if and when you decide to stop working. Increasing your earning power is a discipline, and not a True Wealth asset, because you have to keep working in order for it to be worth anything. Assets may require a modest amount of maintenance energy, such as writing a birthday card to an old friend or attending a board meeting for a nonprofit, but their contribution to your True Wealth is not correlated with the amount of effort they require.

As with traditional assets, the faster you build your True Wealth assets, the earlier you will have the option to slow down or even stop your earning activities. (Although an important part of the SAFE plan is to prioritize making yourself happy and fulfilled now, which suggests finding the kind of work that you enjoy. The more you enjoy your work, the more able you'll be to pursue it in older age, so you will probably be less inclined to stop.)

The SAFE plan calls for developing substantial True Wealth assets in three asset classes: adviser equity, tribe, and savings. You can achieve any quality of life and internal wealth you want with the right mix of these assets, which cannot be said for purely financial assets. Though necessary, the financial components—namely savings and some forms of equity—are often *not* the most important ingredients. Including the nonmonetary assets in your financial planning, described below, allows you to realize substantial "discounts" on the quality of life you want both now and later, because the three asset classes work together to reliably create True Wealth, just as oxygen, fuel, and heat work together to reliably create fire.

THE 1ST TRUE WEALTH ASSET:
Adviser Equity

When you think of *equity*, you probably think of the idea of partial ownership in something. If you have a percentage of equity in your home, you own that percentage free of liens or other claims. If you have a percentage of equity in a company, you own that percentage of the company. To get this equity, you have to make a contribution to the previous owner, usually in the form of cash. In this way, the traditional forms of equity you are familiar with can be bought and sold easily in various marketplaces and do not change in value depending on who holds them.

What we call *adviser equity* is unique for several reasons. First, the contribution that you make in order to earn it is some form of interpersonal contribution—such as advice or mentorship. In some cases, you could consider it to be similar to *sweat equity*, which is equity earned primarily through labor rather than through the investment of capital.

However, the value of sweat equity is often measured by the amount of time you spend improving the value of the property or business multiplied by the going rate for your time. Adviser equity, in contrast, is valued by the degree of impact you make on the future of the property or business and its current owners. A small amount of well-timed advice can have a huge impact on the future, thus creating an opportunity for adviser equity to produce great returns.

The second distinction setting adviser equity apart from other forms is that it can be either formal or informal—meaning, in the latter case, that it doesn't have to be governed by an explicit contract or agreement. When evaluating the progress of your True Wealth, you should consider those who owe you *a debt of gratitude* for your advice and mentorship among your True Wealth assets.

The final distinguishing quality of adviser equity is that it can change wildly in value depending on who holds it. Bryan's brother Tom is a general contractor, and is generally insightful about anything of a mechanical nature. One of his acquaintances was having a particularly troubling problem with his ski boat. A relatively small amount of Tom's free time saved the boat owner many thousands of dollars and turned an embarrassing and expensive backyard project into a weekend of waterskiing with the family. Tom earned *informal* adviser equity, because the boat owner's response to Tom's generosity was in kind: "Tom, anytime you want to use the boat, please just take it out. It's the least I can do." In a few hours, Tom gained access to a financial asset worth more than $60,000. Tom has taken advantage of this offer dozens of times throughout the years, and as a result of his care and attention, the boat is always in tip-top running condition. Given how little boat owners tend to use their boats, Tom's level of access is nearly identical to that of someone who actually paid for it with his own savings.

Unlike sweat equity, Tom's informal adviser equity isn't

transferable. (The offer from the boat owner is specifically for Tom and no one else.) And unlike any financial asset, informal adviser equity tends to be worth *more* the more you spend it. Tom's adviser equity in the boat would likely depreciate over time if he never used it, but each time he uses the boat he also reinforces the relationship—which is the basis for the equity. The cost to maintain this equity and prevent depreciation is the cost of maintaining the relationship, not the cost of maintaining the boat.

Given that not everyone has a gift for troubleshooting broken ski boats, what is the best strategy for maximizing your adviser equity? Imagine you've been following the SAFE plan, and therefore have spent months, years, or even decades honing your ability to be valuable to others in many forms (as we will teach in the coming chapters). Once you've built sufficient momentum in your own ability to be valuable to others, you then have the opportunity to use some of your excess energy and free time in your twenties to fifties with younger people, helping them to increase *their* value to others. Rather than charging money for this service as a paid coach on the side, arrange to share in their lifetime future success via some form of adviser equity.

If your mentee doesn't happen to be the CEO of a high-tech start-up, then asking for formal equity in her future might sound absurd. But if you think of equity not as *ownership* but as *deferred, conditional benefit*, you can find more creative ways to be ultimately compensated for your investment of mentorship.

We call this deferred, conditional benefit "informal equity." Deferred, because you want to earn the benefit during your prime, and receive the benefit later if and when you've decided to slow down. Conditional, because the amount of benefit you'll receive will be based on the degree to which you've helped your mentee increase her earning power and on the degree of gratitude and generosity present in your relationship with her. This form of equity is informal, because the exchange is based on a natural sense of reciprocity among friends and not on binding covenants or agreements.

Think of this form of equity as the ability to call in a favor, either with the explicit expectation of exchange or not. Imagine that a teacher or mentor had made a significant impact on your quality of living, your earning potential, or both. Someone who you would say has really *changed your life.* Might you host him or her in your home for a period of time? Might you offer the use of a vacation home for a month or two? This is the natural sense of reciprocity that comes from informal equity. There is, of course, a limit and unpredictability to this kind of generosity. It would violate the spirit of informal equity to create the feeling of obligation among your friends and mentees. For this reason, it would be very unusual to create True Wealth solely through generosity and reciprocity.

It is common, however, for this kind of equity to vastly improve your sense of luxury and quality of life, just as it did for Tom. Even after just a few years of actively mentoring, helping, and contributing to other people, you'll likely find that you have open invitations to travel to and stay in a variety of cities or even other countries, and to participate for free in a variety of experiences from different sports and hobbies to attending retreats, networking events, and conferences.

Beyond adding to your luxury and quality of life, informal adviser equity gained through generosity and reciprocity also adds to your sense of security in life. Knowing that there are people out there who feel seriously grateful for the help you've provided increases your sense that you'll always have a hand (or many) to help you out if you ever find yourself in a financial pickle. Building this kind of support over decades, in our opinion, is a more valid basis for *true* feelings of security than depending on the markets to continue to rise decade after decade.

The SAFE plan doesn't promise an economy in which every American will retire with at least $3 to $5 million in cash in the bank, which the FACD plan has led you to believe is what you need in order to be happy. The SAFE plan does, however, create opportunities for you to have a very similar True Wealth net worth as those who do, by redeeming adviser equity.

If you've invested in your own ability to be valuable to others, and you look for opportunities to pass on those abilities to younger people, you'll find that your skills are highly relevant for young business leaders and entrepreneurs. Even if you think you have nothing to offer such a business leader today, after a relatively small amount of time and money invested in accordance with the advice throughout this book, you'll be able to develop a specialty that is crucial for the success of a small business or start-up.

When mentoring entrepreneurs, arrange to help them in exchange for *formal* adviser equity: a percentage of ownership in the company. It's formal because it has been converted to a financial instrument that can be sold and transferred into savings, but it's still *adviser* equity because it was earned through interpersonal contribution rather than purchased.

Nathan Otto is an entrepreneur who has founded several companies (including one with Bryan). Three young men starting a company approached him and asked him for mentorship. Nathan agreed and met with them on a regular basis for several months as they faced the normal relationship and business challenges associated with starting a new venture. "There were times where I'm sure I helped them hold the partnership together when it seemed to be on the brink of falling apart," Nathan said of his volunteer contribution to the three. "It was as much about relationship dynamics as about anything directly related to business."

A few months later, Nathan received a surprise. The partnership had recently completed its first product launch, which had gone better than expected. In fact, the three partners had grossed more than $1 million with their first effort. They had gotten together to celebrate their success and decided to thank Nathan for his contribution as an adviser—by awarding him 3 percent equity in the company.

What Tom and Nathan have in common (just about the only thing they have in common) is that they both used their own areas of greatest expertise and interest to give generously in the form of advice and mentorship in that area. In each case there was a modest amount of time investment, and the return was far greater than would be possible by attempting to place a financial value on that time. Both examples started out as *informal* adviser equity because there was no explicit expectation of return. Tom's equity remains *informal,* while Nathan's converted to *formal* adviser equity when he signed the papers awarding him an ownership share in his mentees' company.

The combination of formal adviser equity, which can be converted directly to financial returns, and informal adviser equity, which is the ability to call in specific favors as you need them, works to reduce the cost of living (including during your "retirement") and increase your perception of luxury, security, and happiness.

Just as with any one specific investment, it is unwise to count on the outcome of any one given relationship. Unlike other forms of investment, however, you can change the odds of its working out by increasing your own generosity and your effectiveness at helping others succeed. The better you get at it, the more successful the group of grateful people with whom you hold formal and informal equity becomes. The more of these successful relationships you're able to amass during your working career, the more robust your options will be for a so-called retirement later in life.

If you can't yet see yourself in a mentorship role, don't worry. There are a finite number of skills required to make a business successful, each learnable by virtually anyone. But there is a nearly unlimited demand to bring these skills to bear, particularly among talented and ambitious young people. Every time a young person sets out to accomplish something new, there is an opportunity to earn adviser equity. The more a person accomplishes, the more she attempts, further increasing the demand for high-quality mentorship. This means that there will always be opportunities for every person to improve the future of someone (particularly a younger someone) by sharing well-timed, well-informed advice and mentorship. This means that a finite investment in your ability to mentor someone on a topic related to success yields a self-replenishing field of possible opportunity and rewards.

In this system, young people defer the cost of learning a new skill or accomplishing something new, such as starting a business, by receiving valuable mentorship, experience, knowledge, tools, and advice from older people, without any expense of cash, now or later (unlike with student loans for formal education, where the cash expense of the education accrues for later, with interest!). This advice and mentorship today greatly increases their rate and chance of success, but costs them nothing up front.

On the other side of the exchange, by using informal and formal adviser equity, older people are then able to defer the financial benefit of this value exchange until the time they want to receive benefits without as many time-based commitments. At scale, this cycle creates an economy based on intergenerational generosity and contribution, which automatically distributes value fairly (because projects that receive high-quality advice are more likely to succeed) and is exempt from taxation or any other forms of value extraction (because you can't hoard or tax unrecouped favors) until you convert your adviser equity to savings. It's like a double-tax-free, depreciation-proof, recession-proof retirement account.

THE 2ND TRUE WEALTH ASSET: Tribe

The most self-amplifying and high-leverage of the True Wealth assets is your *tribe*. You can think of tribe as a community of your close friends, all of whom are close with one another, that coalesces around a specific set of values that are most important to you. Your tribe is the source of most of the nonmonetary resources you'll need to create the circumstances of your True Wealth.

Your tribe amplifies your ability to invest in True Wealth disciplines and assets as well as amplifies the positive impact of each discipline on your overall True Wealth. In order to realize the benefits not normally available with the current Western culture's concept of friends or family, we define "tribe" as a group having no fewer than about 15 members, all of whom are close to one another. The largest functioning tribe is likely to be around the maximum number of simultaneous social relationships, which according to the research of evolutionary anthropologist Robin Dunbar is sociobiologically and neurologically capped at around 150 members.[4]

It is possible to have dozens of friends but no tribe. If your friends don't have a similar closeness with one another as they do with you, you lose the network effect of tribe. Much the same way that compartmentalized spending often works at odds with the desired outcome of your entire life system, these individual relationships can end up competing for your time, attention, and adherence to diverse beliefs and values, rather than working collaboratively to produce True Wealth for you. When all of the people you care about most also care about one another, single investments of time and attention can benefit many relationships, like meeting up with a large group of friends for a weekend together rather than having to schedule individual social activities in order to maintain a sense of closeness. Not to mention that anytime you strengthen your relationship with someone, you naturally strengthen your relationships with the people who care about that person most. If the people you care about most all care about one another most, each relationship strengthens all relationships.

It's also possible to have a community of people but no tribe. Communities usually form around a common set of circumstances, a common set of interests, while only tribes form around common sets of values. Communities that form around a common set of circumstances, like a home owners' association, or a common set of interests, like loyalty to a particular sports team, rarely also share a common set of core life values.

Tribes tend to evolve their interpretations of and access to their values together over time. Each member of the tribe can be thought of as an independent researcher, perpetually experimenting and selecting for the best attitudes and behaviors in regard to what they value most. Through natural social interaction, tribes continually share the best results for optimizing for their common values, endlessly iterating on what works best. If you form or find tribe in your lifetime, your participation in that collective social evolutionary process is likely to be one of the deepest, most rewarding components of your True Wealth.

On the material side of the True Wealth equation, tribes provide a lot more than just friendship and crowdsourced research on how to express your most important values (although those benefits are so profound that they would be enough for tribe to earn its place in the SAFE plan).

Tribes share. This has the potential to vastly amplify your

quality of life, financial security, sense of luxury, and True Wealth. For almost everything material that contributes these qualities, the vast majority of the time each material item sits unused. Among the wealthy, sports cars, fancy clothes, expensive jewelry, vacation homes, watercraft of all sizes, private aircraft, and even most of the rooms in the mansion at the center of it all sit unused *almost all the time.* If you ever became wealthy enough to own these items, you could conceivably rent out your convertible turbo Porsche 911 to strangers during the times it was unused, but doing so would likely decrease your felt sense of True Wealth.

No matter what kind of car you own, however, if you let one of your most beloved friends borrow it when he or she is visiting from out of town, it tends to *increase* your sense of True Wealth. For this reason, tribe transforms True Wealth assets, so they don't require that you bear the full cost of ownership in order to derive the full benefit to your True Wealth. Since your True Wealth is in part determined by your capacity to reliably and continually create the circumstances that lead to internal wealth, the SAFE plan values these assets by their effect on that capacity rather than by their ownership value on a balance sheet. For example, an *invitation* to tour the country in a friend's luxury RV would be a much bigger True Wealth asset than an *owned* RV sitting neglected and accumulating repair costs, even though the exact opposite is true from a traditional asset value point of view.

Tribe is a constantly renewable source of these kinds of invitations. Of course, *someone* in the tribe needs to buy the RV in order for the members to add it to their True Wealth "balance sheet," and you might not currently know anyone with enough financial resources to make that purchase. But it doesn't take very many of these purchases for a tribe to start to feel a lot wealthier, and if the cost of ownership is shared among 20, 50, 100, or even 150 people, a few key luxury items that are consistent with creating the circumstances that enhance the tribe's core values start to feel a lot more within reach.

In addition to reducing the cost of ownership of many of the emotional triggers for financial abundance and True Wealth, tribe also reduces the downside risks in life. It acts as a form of insurance. Support for the unforeseen challenges, setbacks, or needs of tribe members is naturally distributed among the tribe. If a tribe member gets evicted, loses her job, or has an unexpected medical bill, it may be too large a burden to expect an individual friendship to help make up the gap. But shared among dozens of tribe members, those setbacks can seem almost trivial. These risks are significantly less scary when they are distributed and absorbed across a wide community of people, enhancing the tribe's emotional sense of financial security—a critical aspect of True Wealth.

Tribe doesn't reduce just the downside risk associated with unforeseen problems, but also the downside of riskier self-investments like starting a new company. We have a dear friend in our tribe who for the last two years has been living with friends in the community for stretches ranging from a week to a couple of months. He's not homeless out of destitution or bad luck. He's choosing to eliminate as many expenses as possible because he is trying a start-up business idea, but he didn't have the capital to be able to take off work to do it without changing his monthly financial obligations. By essentially eliminating his living expenses, he was able to use that time to launch his start-up. Obviously not *everyone* in our tribe can do that at the same time, but the tribe has enough "couches" so that a few people can be doing it at any time. Because two of our tribe's core values are *self-expression* and *contribution*, we believe in his business idea and we were excited to participate in making it happen. Some people have the option of living at home with Dad or borrowing some of Mom's money to start a company, but unlike forming or joining a tribe, that option is not available to everyone.

Before the invention of insurance, geographic communities filled the role of tribe with respect to lowering risk. If your neighbor's farm burned down, you got to work, donating as much time, money, resources, and attention as you could spare to get him back on his feet; in exchange, you got the assurance (and "insurance"!) that if the same or a similar accident happened to you, your neighbor would be there to help you.

In the new global culture, we collectively place a much lower value on "being neighborly," and in return have gained much more access to choosing our friends based on values rather than geography. We now have the opportunity to distribute these risks among an even larger group, and on the basis of love and caring.

The right tribe has so many systemic benefits, it's like super-food for your True Wealth. It amplifies your returns in each aspect of the SAFE plan, and reduces your cost of investment. Assuming that your tribe's values are consistent with the values of the SAFE plan, such as contribution and self-investment, then just spending time with your friends is likely to be the cheapest and most powerful way to invest in the other True Wealth disciplines and assets.

Your ability and proclivity to practice Systemic Spending would be significantly lower without a tribe, because you would lose the benefit of the experimentation and learning process of each other tribe member. And your Happiness Exchange Rate would be lower, because spending time with tribe is more rewarding and systemically beneficial than simply hanging out with a friend. Your tribe automatically stores and shares the collective best wisdom about how to be happy, because sharing and expressing your most important values with people you love is what will likely make you the happiest.

Tribe is also a natural spring of opportunities to invest in your value to others, as well as opportunities to capitalize on that investment in the form of potential business partnerships and job opportunities. In much the same way, tribe maximizes your exposure to potential formal and informal adviser equity opportunities and helps match your most developed skills to the needs of any of the people in any of the personal networks of the tribe members.

Assuming everyone in the community is engaged in their own version of the SAFE plan, there is a synergistic effect of everyone all learning the most important valuable life skills. Because people who belong to a group tend to specialize in different skills, a tribe of people dedicated to investing in themselves will soon become a network of informal mentors for just about every relevant and marketable skill. The value of membership in a given tribe appreciates over time, because as everyone contributes to one another, learning to be more and more valuable, the value you can give to and receive from each member of that community keeps going up and up.

Tribe also can be a repository for informal equity. If the majority of the informal equity you've created is based on one-off contributions you've made to people who don't know one another, they won't be aware of the contributions you've made to others. The most value you can redeem is the value of each individual favor. A tribe stores the collective knowledge of all the contributions you've made within the tribe. Therefore, when you start to build informal equity within a tribe, you develop and maintain a reputation for a specific flavor of contribution, which you can easily leverage to gain more opportunities to be valuable to others, or even redeem informal equity *before* you earn it with a specific person.

For a community of friends to yield the super-food benefits of tribe, it must conform to a specific formula, which we detail in chapter 8 of this book. Like all aspects of the SAFE plan, it does require focus and attention, but we believe it is well within reach of all but the most socially challenged members of society.

THE 3RD TRUE WEALTH ASSET: **Savings**

Once you need to spend less to be happier, due to an increased Happiness Exchange Rate, and once your earnings power has gone up, the resulting difference between the two is what allows you to save: often much more than you'd be able to save on lower earnings, by "pinching pennies" rather than increasing your earnings and your Happiness Exchange Rate.

At first glance, you might confuse the SAFE plan's message of deriving more happiness so you can spend less with the FACD message of forcing yourself to spend less. What makes the SAFE plan more plausible is the timing of *when* you save. In this model of savings, you reduce your spending only *in response* to achieved happiness and satisfaction, instead of prior to that point. Willpower is not a factor. If you invest in your earning potential via your value to other people and your Happiness Exchange Rate simultaneously, you'll find that you automatically feel like spending less money, because you don't have as many of the negative feelings for which normal spending is compensating. This effect, when combined with increased income, which comes from investing in your earning potential via value to others, leaves a more and more comfortable margin available to commit to savings.

In order to experience the financial freedom associated with True Wealth, you must have some financial resources that are not dependent on your relationship with any other person or organization. Savings is what you spend later in life when you may want fewer time-based commitments and obligations. Therefore investing in your True Wealth also means setting aside some of your income for savings.

Once you save the money, however, you must *really* save it, rather than try to reinvest it by chasing higher returns. Many people think that a 401(k) plan, home equity, or mutual fund is a form of savings. This is a greatly misguided view. These are investments, and subject to the same risks as all investments.

Our view is, you should not risk money simply to get more money (as in stock investments). The money you risk (in the form of investing in yourself, as described in this book) should be in service of something that will improve *you*, further your purpose, as well as increase your income. The thing to do with money that isn't being invested in yourself is to save it for real, in a boring savings account, or in CDs or money market accounts, or perhaps in inflation-adjusted bonds. Savings, to the extent you have them, should be boring.

A lifetime of investing in your Happiness Exchange Rate, and your adviser equity, combined with focusing your earning power on the kind of work that itself is fulfilling and rewarding (and that you will want to continue longer), will drive down significantly the actual cash requirements of a lifestyle filled with your most cherished experiences. How much you *need* to save is up to you. The SAFE plan doesn't replace the need for savings, but it does *reduce* the need for savings. One measure of your net True Wealth is the ease with which savings comes to you *combined* with your sense that the amount you need to have saved in order to feel free and satisfied is continually shrinking (even as the balance of your savings continually grows).

SYSTEMS WITHIN SYSTEMS

The same systems thinking that makes Systemic Spending self-amplifying also makes the entire SAFE plan self-amplifying. Take any component of the system, and by improving it, you positively impact all of the other components. For example, a better Happiness Exchange Rate makes you more valuable to others (because you're more pleasant and inspiring to be around), makes you more effective at Systemic Spending (because you have more self-awareness of how each act of spending affects other contexts), and also makes you more desirable as a tribe member.

Your financial ecosystem is also amplified by the financial ecosystem of every other person with whom you interact. The fact that True Wealth separates capacity from ownership makes the SAFE plan a fundamentally cooperative one, rather than a competitive one. This means that the more successful your friends are at their SAFE plans, the more opportunities for success you have in your own SAFE plan. The more adviser equity, tribe, and value to others each tribe collectively develops, the more beneficial it will be to other tribes, and vice versa. The more True Wealth each individual has, the more True Wealth is available to everyone on the planet, because True Wealth calls for ever more reduction in redundancies and more efficient utilization of shared resources, and also for a better harmonization of the interests, needs, and capabilities between older and younger generations. Not on a legislated basis, but rather on the basis of the depth of caring between friends. This additive network effect can scale globally and intergenerationally, as we all collectively use external wealth more and more efficiently to reinforce our internal wealth.

Most important, the SAFE plan is designed to make you feel, well, *safe*—at every step of the way.

"WHY DO YOU THINK THIS WORKS?"

This book presents a complete plan of investment, the SAFE plan, which we promote (and which we ourselves follow) as a full alternative to the FACD plan. While it can yield results for people starting even in their fifties, the best results (as with any financial plan) will come to those who invest in this plan over many decades.

This may lead to a natural question on the part of the reader: "If you're recommending we follow this plan over decades, where are the examples of people who have done so and succeeded?" This is an important and fair question, and it deserves to be addressed head-on.

Our recommendations in this book are all investments we ourselves have made (and we have seen many of our friends make) over the last decade, and have seen ROI—both financial and nonfinancial—in the time frame of six months to ten years. However, we can't point to an example of one person who has followed this plan from college graduation through retirement.

Why not? Because we are pioneering an alternative to an investment and retirement model that has proven itself completely broken and bankrupt only in the last ten to twenty years. We and our friends started noticing this wreckage and exploring alternatives in our own lives.

What you are about to read in these pages is not some theory we made up sitting in our chairs. It has been our lived reality, and the lived reality of our tribe of about 150 friends—entrepreneurs and employees alike, mostly in our late thirties and early forties, in a wide variety of industries, from the most techie to the most mundane, based mostly in the Bay Area and New York City, for the past decade.

We started to notice that we, and most people in our tribe, did not seem to have the same problems that others were facing during the last fifteen years of economic turmoil in the United States. Our earning power was steadily rising, while other people were stagnating, getting laid off, or going through long periods of unemployment. Our costs were going down (and therefore our savings up) as we pioneered ways to live in communities that felt like a plus in our lives, not a minus. The parents in our tribe started coming together to support one another, building networks and communities of care that had everyone feeling more safe and secure about the future, not less.

A few people in our tribe have created enough financial wealth to "retire" in their twenties, thirties, and forties, but that was not the focus of their efforts, nor of anyone else we know; even those we know who could retire don't, as they love their work. However, for everyone in our tribe, including the majority who continue to rely on their own earning power, we noticed that they do not have the same level of panic, dread, or low-level anxiety about their economic future that is pervasive in the surrounding culture. Collectively we had discovered something important, and we wanted to share it with the wider world. This book is that sharing.

CHAPTER 1

INVESTING TO INCREASE YOUR HAPPINESS EXCHANGE RATE

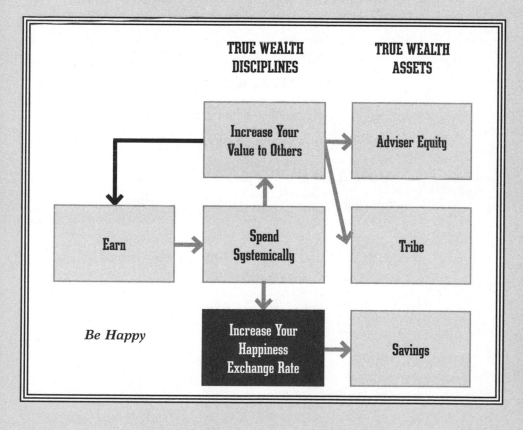

- GET A DISCOUNT ON THE CIRCUMSTANCES THAT MAKE YOU HAPPY
- GET GOOD AT PREDICTING WHAT MAKES YOU HAPPY
- ENJOY THE EXPERIENCES YOU'RE ALREADY HAVING
- TREAT NEGATIVE FEELINGS AT THE ROOT
- FOCUS ON FINDING AND LIVING YOUR PURPOSE

ALEXANDER AND THE QUITE NICE BOTTLE

In 2012, at the age of twenty-three, investment banker and foreign exchange trader Alex Hope earned a dubious distinction: in one night of drinking and partying at the Playground nightclub in Liverpool, he racked up what the media reported as the largest bar tab in history.

Buying rounds for strangers in the bar (particularly female strangers) that night, he eventually ordered forty bottles of Ace of Spades champagne at $795 each, and a single premium bottle at $38,000. Not satisfied with that extravagance, he then decided to order the most expensive bottle of champagne in the world. Weighing in at ninety-nine pounds, this Ace of Spades bottle had to be carried out by two waiters. That added $200,000 to the tab. He shared this with his friends and some soccer and reality TV stars who happened to be in the bar. The total bar tab, including gratuity, came to around $330,000.[1]

Asked by *The Huffington Post* why he wanted to buy a $200,000 bottle of champagne, he said: "People like Jay Z have bought it. . . . And I thought to myself, 'I never treat myself, I don't have a flashy car, but if I go out [and] buy this bottle,' and for me it will be like an achievement thing. . . . I think only three or four people in the world have ever bought that, so for me to be the youngest it's like really neat. I told you, Jay Z's bought it and to be associated with someone like that just by buying a bottle of champagne is quite nice."[2]

Hope's expensive night out raises a few questions. Do you really need to spend $330,000 to have an experience that you end up evaluating as "like really neat" and "quite nice"? Could such a modest level of pleasure possibly be had at a cheaper price—perhaps with a picnic under a tree with a few friends?

These questions cut to the heart of the Happiness Exchange Rate. The basic idea is this:

The more you must spend money in order to be happy, the more expensive that happiness is.

Just as countries have a rate by which their forms of money can be exchanged—called a currency exchange rate—you have an exchange rate by which you exchange money for happiness.

That doesn't mean that money "buys" you happiness. But if you and a person named John each spend $65,000 per year, and you are wildly happier than John, then you are getting a lot more happiness per dollar you spend. Not 100 percent of your spending led directly to your happiness (just as nowhere near 100 percent of business expenses lead directly to profit). But you are getting more "happiness mileage" out of the money you *do* spend; your Happiness Exchange Rate is higher.

Given that happiness is one of the top reasons people give for wanting to earn more money, focusing on improving your Happiness Exchange Rate is one of the wisest investments you could make, helping you get more of what you want out of life with less effort and expenditure. But is it possible to *invest* in your Happiness Exchange Rate?

Yes. Any time or money you spend that allows you to derive more happiness for less money and effort in the future is an investment in your Happiness Exchange Rate. This chapter will give specific instructions on how to do so. The payoff, in terms of increased happiness (internal wealth) and decreased expenses (external wealth), can be dramatic.

The latter benefit of such investments—decreased expenses—is what allows for stress-free savings in the SAFE plan. We do not encourage you to scrimp and save, in a miserly (and miserable) fashion. Instead, throughout this book we will encourage you to invest in earning more money. In this chapter, however, we start with the idea of investing to get more happiness from the money you do earn, so that you need to spend less of it. Once you need to spend less to be happy, and once you are earning more (discussed in the rest of the book), then savings—a crucial part of any financial plan—becomes naturally aligned with your behavior and your natural desires.

THE TRAGEDY OF GOAL SETTING

In order to increase your Happiness Exchange Rate, you will have to get away from the idea that you should set and reach some kind of financial "goal," such as earning $100,000 per year or having $1,000,000 in the bank, and that you should sacrifice much of your happiness now in order to reach that goal.

Much of how we manage our personal financial lives is derived from what we as a culture have learned from business in the last one hundred years of the Industrial Age. Robust systems and thought processes were developed over many decades to handle the complex, risk-allergic task of managing and protecting large organizations. Because they seemed to work so well, smart people applied these same thought processes to small, entrepreneurial ventures, and eventually they trickled down to the individual. Though much good has come from borrowing best practices from business and applying them to individuals, perhaps the most pronounced—and most dangerous—of these practices is the idea of *personal goal setting.*

How could we possibly describe something as wholesome as goal setting as "dangerous"?

In order to formulate a high-quality goal, most highly paid coaches and consultants will tell you that the goal must be specific and measurable. In the 1990s, "SMART" goals became very popular, based on variations of the acronym "Specific, Measurable, Achievable, Relevant, and Time-Bound." Therefore, in the goal-setting process, the first step is to take your desired outcome and express it in as tangible a way as possible. Because all meaningful goals have an important *interior* or emotional component, this means that on some level you are converting your *interior* desired state into an *exterior* result that you think will help you achieve your interior state. This is logical, especially if you intend to collaborate with another person on achieving your goal. After all, how are you supposed to know if you are on track if you can't express your goal in a tangible, exterior, specific, and measurable way? So, to the best of your ability, you make that translation and restate your goal. Instead of "I want to look and feel great," you create the goal "I want to lose ten pounds." Instead of "I want to feel financially free," you create the goal "I want to earn $100,000."

That alone isn't necessarily problematic (assuming you are competent at predicting what exterior results actually lead to your desired interior state—a pretty big assumption). But what commonly happens next is often directly counterproductive to your actual intent. Once you've stated your goal, your attention turns to decisions and activities that optimize for achieving that specific external goal, regardless of how those decisions and activities may affect the entire system. The connection of the goal to the entire system is lost in an attempt to focus on achieving the goal itself. This may work for some businesses, but it is dreadful when making important decisions about how to spend your time and money to create a life you love.

This is why so many slave away at jobs they hate, working up to eighty hours per week, even giving up holidays and weekends to try to meet a financial goal of earning $100,000 per year—which was meant to be an expression of the internal state of financial freedom. Giving up freedom as a strategy to get freedom. The insanity of these types of strategies is a result of overoptimization, valuing the tangible evidence that is supposed to represent an interior state more than the interior state itself. For most people, this disconnect then makes it nearly impossible to continue to pursue the goal wholeheartedly, and a schism appears in their minds.

This is a typical story of that schism:

You believe that you need the $100,000 salary (or $X in the bank, or so much in "passive income," or whatever is true for you) in order to feel financially free. As you work toward that freedom, the nature of the work itself erodes more and more of your experience of freedom. When you reach your threshold for "pain" with regard to lack of freedom, you pull back from work. When you fail to reach your goal, you blame yourself for pulling back. You say things to yourself like "If I had only pulled an all-nighter before that big deadline I might have gotten the promotion." You attribute more value to the goal than to your feelings, because after all, "no pain, no gain," right? You redouble your commitment to your goal and swear to yourself that you'll work harder next time, and be willing to forgo even *more* freedoms. But again, when you reach your limit of how much freedom you are willing to go without, you pull back again. You self-diagnose as having a problem with your *motivation*, because you can't make yourself do what you know is good for you.

If this story resonates for you (in any area of your life—health, love, sex, etc.), then you've misdiagnosed yourself. The problem isn't your *motivation*, it's your definition of what you are supposed to be motivated to do. It's a good thing you aren't more "motivated" to achieve your goals, otherwise you'd risk sacrificing every last bit of freedom, happiness, and health to try to achieve the internal experience that you would have utterly depleted. The problem is compartmentalization and overoptimization. A numerical goal like $100,000 per year of income cannot describe the complexity of your life's whole system.

Michael interviewed John Mackey, CEO of Whole Foods, and coauthor (with Raj Sisodia) of *Conscious Capitalism*, on systems thinking and overoptimization: "The way most people approach business—and the way they mostly teach in business school—involves the analytical mind. It divides it up and looks at parts in isolation. In contrast, in our work, we're trying to show how everything fits together in the larger system. You have to manage the system. Most good leaders intuitively know this, they're just not conscious of it. They understand that they've got to take care of their customers. They get that their employees can't take care of the customers well if their employees aren't flourishing. And they get that they need to treat their suppliers well, which provide them everything they don't produce themselves."[3]

Most businesses measure only one metric—profit. But there are clearly times when the needs of key suppliers, customers, employees, company culture, or the greater community seem to be at odds with profit. Ignoring these needs over the long term would of course be disastrous. Leaders of these organizations must think systemically and optimize for the health of the entire system, or else the profit motive itself will end up destroying profitability in the long term.

Goals, when used properly, can be a fantastic tool. The useful purpose of goals is to clarify and communicate your future direction. Once the direction is clear, and all the people affected by the goal are on the same page, then it has served its purpose and should be valued *less* than the systemic outcomes it was created to produce. Rather than a single metric, what we really want for ourselves is a complex array of different goals and values. These work together to form an *aesthetic* much the way a particular artist forms her unique style.

An aesthetic is a precisely chosen balance among effort, reward, ease, challenge, growth, satisfaction, freedom, commitments, and dozens of other important values. When any one of these is given too much emphasis, the aesthetic is diminished or destroyed, like a movie with too much emphasis on camera angles or a cocktail party with too much emphasis on the creativity of the bartender. Those are important elements, but are best when in the proper relationship to the other elements.

The happiness you get out of your spending will increase when all or most of your expenditures go toward the particular aesthetic of happiness you are trying to create—rather than trying to "buy" happiness with a big blowout payday at the end of your career, once you've reached your "goals." The discipline we recommend to create just the right aesthetic in your life, the one with the most happiness for the least money, is Systemic Spending.

In order to use Systemic Spending effectively, you must consciously choose your aesthetic for how you want to live your life, so that you can determine whether purchases enhance or detract from the overall aesthetic. To do this, simply start to pay attention to the silent ways you approve and disapprove of the people around you and their choices. (Your approval and disapproval of yourself is often too wrapped up in insecurities and other out-of-date stories about yourself to be a totally accurate guide.)

Notice when you think someone is being too flashy, or working too hard, or not working hard enough, or spending too much on entertainment, or suffering in a crummy apartment when he or she obviously could afford something more suitable. These thoughts are your clues to the outlines of your own aesthetic. Replace your goals of being rich with a clear aesthetic of comfort, freedom, contribution, and influence. Then notice how making different choices about how to spend your time and money either support or detract from that aesthetic. From there you can start to improve the quality of the decisions that you make, because your motivation and good decision making will be applied to creating a financial ecosystem in your life, with a particular aesthetic, rather than a compartmentalized metric.

BREEDING LOW-QUALITY DECISIONS

Bad spending decisions start with how you relate to spending itself. The interior, emotional relationship that most people have with spending and investing is an unhealthy tug-of-war that limits your ability to successfully invest in yourself and think about spending systemically.

The idea of *spending* and the idea of *investing*, as they are usually held, have an adversarial relationship. They are in competition for a finite resource, namely your money. Most of us believe that we must choose between the two with each dollar that accumulates in our bank accounts. As a result, many people live their lives perpetually suspended in a moral dilemma between the saving and investing they *should* do and the spending and consuming they *want* to do.

You may feel caught in a catch-22: you don't have as much money as you'd like now, but in order to grow more money in the future, you'll have to save and invest now, even though you already feel like you don't have enough money to buy what you want now. Your financial life may be full of shame: you know what you are "supposed" to do—save—yet you so frequently fail to do it. You may feel as if you have a split personality around money.

Sometimes you are a Dr. Jekyll of self-repression, other times you are a Mr. Hyde of uncontrolled shopping and splurging. To buy an item, especially an expensive item, when caught in this internal conflict, we must face questions like "Do I deserve it?," "Do I lack self-control if I spend this money?," and "Am I a bad person if I do what I want instead of what I should do?" These are extremely low-quality questions for making decisions. It's as if we engage an emotionally immature part of the brain that is incapable of long-term planning and calculating probabilities.

Since Systemic Spending is the discipline of bringing investment thinking to bear on ordinary expenditures, the kinds of questions you ask yourself when you are considering a purchase are incredibly important. Imagine the disastrous outcome if Warren Buffett and Charlie Munger—the world's most recognized billionaire investors—decided which investments to make by asking themselves those low-quality questions. They would certainly be bankrupt several times over. It's true that these investors are considering which insurance *company* to buy, rather than the more mundane consideration of which insurance *policy* to buy, but we could still learn a lot from the high-quality questions that successful investors ask themselves.

For example, when you are considering a purchase, ask yourself high-quality questions that investors like Warren and Charlie might ask themselves: "Based on the best information available to me, what are the most probable long-term effects of buying this item?"; "How will this purchase affect all of the different contexts in my life?"; "How will this expenditure increase my value to others?"; "How can I use this item to further my underlying agendas for self-improvement, contribution, and awareness?" When you approach each spending decision this way, you will likely come to the conclusion that systemic spending now is often a *better* investment than saving and putting the savings into traditional investment vehicles. After all, what stock, security, commodity, or currency can actually add value to *you* when you buy it?

HOW TO INVEST IN YOUR HAPPINESS EXCHANGE RATE

Your Happiness Exchange Rate consists of four distinct skills.

H.E.R. SKILL #1: Use Systemic Spending to Get a Discount on the Circumstances That Make You Happy

We both know a couple, whom we'll call James and Selena, who love each other very much, who are wealthy individually and as a couple, and who live in a posh home. They enjoy all the accoutrements of their wealth: fine dining, travel, entertaining at home, attendance at marvelous arts and charity events. However, until recently they spent a good deal of their time fighting. If you recall any period when you've been consistently fighting with a significant other, you know it makes everything else you might be doing together (restaurants, travel, entertainment) provide essentially zero happiness. It can even make your time apart during the day miserable, as you stew over the thing the other person said as you were heading out the door.

Thus, for James and Selena, their Happiness Exchange Rate was basically zero. They were miserable, no matter how much money they spent.

James and Selena finally decided to get help for their relationship. It turned out they were triggering deep wounds in each other that hadn't healed since their childhoods. They invested in couples therapy and also individual therapy to work on their issues. After about half a year of this investment, they were doing much better as a couple. They had stopped fighting so much, and were each beginning to feel much better about themselves, and about their future together.

From a compartmentalized spending perspective, they were spending a lot of money on this therapy—more than a thousand dollars per month in individual and couples therapy. Even to a wealthy person, that may seem like a lot to spend on improving just one area of one's personal life.

But seen from a Systemic Spending perspective, this spending was a bargain. They had "won" the investment game from the FACD perspective, but when it came time to convert those winnings to happiness (the final step in the game), they lost much of their "winnings." They were spending more than ten thousand dollars per month living their lifestyle with their FACD winnings, and getting almost no happiness in return.

Now, by investing what was for them a relatively small amount in this one area, every other area of their spending yielded improvements. Restaurant meals and trips that would have previously yielded almost no happiness (because they were fighting) were now joyous occasions for them to experience and express their love together. They both came to their work lives with more zest and vitality. Their Happiness Exchange Rate went through the roof.

You might think that this example doesn't apply if you don't live at such a high level of material comfort, or if you're not having relationship problems, or if you can't afford psychotherapy to fix a relationship. But the fundamental point of this example applies to almost everyone, in every circumstance: your general mood greatly influences your Happiness Exchange Rate, and there are many things you can do, small and large, to invest in improving the circumstances that lead to your consistently being in a better mood.

In general, you will be in a better mood if you have better health and fitness. You will be in a better mood if you have stronger and richer social ties. You will be in a better mood if you feel more secure in your earning power. You will be in a better mood if your work feels aligned with your purpose and mission. These are all things you can invest in, as we'll continue to show you throughout this book. As your mood improves, the amount of happiness you get from any given expenditure improves, and thus your Happiness Exchange Rate (as well as the ease with which you are able to cut back spending and save) improves as well.

Many people are wary of spending money on things like therapy or personal development workshops, and these can often cost thousands of dollars. Such spending may seem like a luxury—but it can be a huge leverage point on all the other money you're spending. If you could spend a few thousand dollars and improve the return you get on all your other investments, you wouldn't consider that a luxury. This may not be possible in the realm of traditional FACD investing, but it is frequently possible when investing in yourself. If the aim of investing, ultimately, is to secure happiness for yourself and others, then anything that allows you to get much more happiness out of the experiences you currently spend money on is a good investment.

H.E.R. SKILL #2: Get Good at Predicting What Makes You Happy

Think of all your purchases as serving two functions:

1. Providing whatever benefit you seek from the purchase directly.
2. Serving as an experiment about how happy that purchase, or type of purchase, makes you, and how happy similar purchases are likely to make you in the future.

A great deal of the value of any given purchase comes from the second function, as this allows you to hone your purchasing in the future, toward the highest Happiness Exchange Rate possible.

If you were able to recapture the full monetary value of all the items you've purchased over decades that ended up giving you little or no lasting happiness or value, you might have several hundred thousand dollars, or more, in the bank right now.

One of the most important aspects of becoming good at this skill is noticing how each purchase affects *all* contexts of your life, systemically, over long periods of time. You can begin to notice how certain purchases don't provide much happiness over time, over many different contexts, while others pack a punch over time, and over multiple contexts in your life. Become a good hunter for happiness bargains, where the value you are getting from the purchase, over time, and over different areas of your life, far outweighs the price.

H.E.R. SKILL #3: Improve Your Ability to Enjoy the Experiences You're Already Having

Many people develop a low Happiness Exchange Rate because they are unable to enjoy the experiences they're actually having. They're unable to enjoy these experiences because they're not paying attention. In some sense, they're not actually having the experience they're paying for. They are not *present*. When you are eating at a restaurant, for example, consider the difference in your enjoyment (and the value you are getting for your money) between being present for the enjoyment of the meal versus thinking about the e-mails you need to send tomorrow at work.

You may previously have thought of presence as basically having nothing to do with your retirement plan. But when you consider how much money you've wasted in your life not enjoying experiences you've paid for, it's actually an essential part.

Presence can be cultivated systematically. People have been doing it for thousands of years with various forms of meditation and yoga. Even if meditation seems too spiritual or religious for you, there are now many secular, nonspiritual, nonreligious ways to learn simple practices that increase your focus and presence. If you search online for classes in meditation or mindfulness, you will no doubt find many in any metropolitan area. You can also find recorded or virtual classes in meditation.

Investing in increasing your presence greatly increases the enjoyment you get out of the experiences you are having. It also allows you to get more and more enjoyment out of simpler experiences. Contentment will come a lot cheaper for you, allowing you to spend less and save more.

H.E.R. SKILL #4: Learn to Treat Negative Feelings at the Root, Not with Retail Therapy

Often when we're feeling bad, we think that not feeling bad is the same as feeling good, so we reach for things that will numb our feelings or help us escape from them. The skill of knowing the difference, and sticking with and feeling the unpleasant feelings until you can resolve them, is a huge factor in the Happiness Exchange Rate. It could be counterintuitive that experiencing negative feelings is a key to happiness, but our observation of ourselves and others shows that you can't selectively numb feelings. If you are numbing the pain, you're also, in the long run, numbing your capacity for joy. While there's a time and a place for having a drink after a rough day at work, most people vastly overestimate the effectiveness, and underestimate the costs, of habitual attempts to anesthetize negative feelings with drinking, drugs, sex, or shopping.

The root of these recurring negative emotions is usually a negative belief about yourself. "I'm not good enough." Treating negative feelings at the root means excavating those negative beliefs and allowing them to be loved by you and by others. You do not need to have been traumatized as a child to walk around with persistent feelings of not being good enough, or not fitting in, or not feeling worthy of being loved deeply for who you are. These persistent negative feelings are common human experiences. Oftentimes, people seek to paper over these feelings via money and the things money can buy.

Such attempts can get quite elaborate, involving dreams of happiness and love to be found in, for example, real estate, cars, vacations, gadgets, toys, and fashion. But if you're seeking to fill a void in your heart via external purchases, actually you've discovered a black hole into which money is poured but never escapes. Dealing with the feelings directly is much more economical in the long run. As our friend Victor Cheng, a coach for executives of rapidly growing start-ups, says, "Psychotherapy is cheaper than retail therapy."

H.E.R. SKILL #5: Focus on Finding and Living Your Purpose, Not on Increasing Comfort

For the past fifty years or more, the primary promises of consumerism and technology have been *comfort* and *convenience*, and boy, have they delivered. Such iconic marketing slogans as "You deserve a break today" and "Leave the driving to us" reinforce the idea that the secret to being happy is having less to do. In order to reach this lazy man's utopia, all one needed to do was to secure a steady flow of "disposable" income, and then actually dispose of it by purchasing as many consumer products as possible, and enjoy the good (if not active) life.

This created a new sense of purpose en masse for Americans. Get that cash so you can buy the next automatic thus-and-such. A few generations earlier, in the 1920s and '30s, many U.S. workers were leaving farms and rural areas for urban areas to work in dismal factories. Your best chance of "getting ahead" was still to apprentice as a craftsman—say as a cobbler—and then work over the course of several years or decades under the tutelage of your master craftsman to become the best cobbler you could be. The reputation of the quality of your work would spread and your own hard work would ensure your survival. Whether through farm work, factory work, or craftsmanship, for most it was a hard life. No wonder the messages touting benefits that you could reap "from the comfort of your own home" found their audience a few decades later. But in the shift from *survival via craft* to *get that cash* something vital to happiness was lost. A sense of purpose.

Purpose is an *infinite* value. That is to say, a deeper, more profound sense of purpose is always *infinitely* available. Money is a *finite* value. In other words, it is very useful, up to a point, and then getting more stops being necessary (or even desirable). If you have enough money to buy what you want in order to create the experience you want—such as love, or family, or belonging— it is more satisfying to turn your attention *away* from earning more money and *toward* actually creating the experience. (*Comfort* and *convenience* are both finite values.)

This mismatch—finite versus infinite—makes "getting more money" a very poor candidate for a satisfying purpose, and yet it occupies that spot in the consciousness of most people participating in first-world culture today, like a dirty napkin saving your seat at dinner.

Culturally, we've long since reached our sense of sufficiency around comfort and convenience, which is why you rarely hear these benefits being hawked in contemporary ads. So comfort's out, but the means of getting there—the money—is still firmly in place as the unifying and unsatisfying purpose for the first world.

But a sense of purpose—of commitment to something greater than ourselves—is one of life's greatest opportunities for happiness and satisfaction. As is the slow unfolding process of self-discovery required to find and pursue it. To capture this opportunity (which also happens to radically improve your Happiness Exchange Rate), you'll have to admit that your actual value of sufficiency for money is much less than you've previously believed. You are likely pretty resistant to the idea of giving up on the idea of having a lot of money. Understandably so, because money is also a symbol of freedom, prestige, power, influence, and a host of other desirable experiences.

We want you to discover, through self-experimentation and making the kinds of investments recommended throughout this book, that you can actually gain *more* freedom, prestige, power, influence, happiness, satisfaction, and just about any other experience you want by investing in and creating those experiences *directly.* Start to shift your focus away from "How much can I get?" (a money question) and toward "What do I have to give?" (a purpose question). From that place, you can begin to explore what value, what experiences, what services you most enjoy contributing to others. What would you gladly supply even if there were no financial compensation at all? This is an inquiry into your purpose.

The path to discovering or refining your purpose is to examine which of your contributions to others feels most significant and free. Follow that thread of thinking, and invest in any activity that your purpose suggests—usually, some form of being of service to others, even if that service is expressed primarily in your workplace (and not, say, feeding the hungry in Africa, which is often the kind of thing people think of in association with the word "purpose"). Over time, you'll lift the curse of comfort and start to follow your purpose to be of service to others—at which point, ironically, the increase in value that you are providing globally in your life is most likely to convert into a much greater source of revenue and income for you.

$3 MILLION DOWN THE DRAIN

To see the power of the Happiness Exchange Rate (and in this example, the first H.E.R. Skill of Systemic Spending) in action, consider the story of two different couples we know who recently bought expensive homes. While this example is about two couples who are relatively well off, the basic principles apply at nearly any wealth or income level above mere subsistence.

Both couples recently had sizable financial windfalls, and they decided to spare no expense (each ended up buying a home for about $3 million) and get the home "they've always dreamed of."

The first couple, whom we'll call Derek and Anne, traveled to the world's most exotic locations to find a home that would represent "the good life." They wanted something that looked amazing, had the finest appointments and appliances, and impressive views. They confided in Bryan that when they were shopping for houses, a key factor was how impressed they thought their friends and families would be. In other words, they viewed their purchase one-dimensionally, and evaluated potential homes on the basis of the quality of the home itself. Derek has experience in real estate, so he made sure that they didn't overpay when they selected a mansion in St. Barts, a picturesque tropical island and favorite vacation spot for celebrities and the social elite.

The second couple, whom we'll call Matt and Erica, had a very different agenda. They wanted to create an environment that was fertile for enhancing their creativity and growth, and for strengthening their sense of community, all the while raising their children among friends and family. They lived in New York, but they had friends all over the country and even the world. The largest concentration of friends was in San Rafael in Northern California, so they decided they would commit first to that location. For Matt and Erica, a community of inspiring friends is the source of creative projects, great parties, and even business partnerships (Matt is a successful entrepreneur who had just sold his business).

When they asked themselves, "What's the life we dream of?," they imagined a constant flow of people they love in the house, challenging them to grow, supporting them as they try new things, helping them to raise their two children by providing a diverse set of positive role models. In other words, they saw the value of a new home in terms of how it would affect every *other* area of their lives—how it would affect the aesthetic of the entire system. (This is the essence of Systemic Spending.) So they decided to invite six of their friends (including two other entrepreneurs who had sold successful businesses and several self-development experts) to live with them as roommates.

Financially they didn't need roommates, as they were contemplating buying a $3 million mansion for cash. But living together with friends they love, whom they refer to as "chosen family," is a perfect expression of their ideal aesthetic. When they decided on which property to buy, their considerations were not about appliance quality and impressive views. They were looking for a layout that would allow for four couples to live together and have the right mix of privacy, autonomy, and community. They looked for homes with large plots of land, and zoning laws that would allow them to build structures like small offices or even additional bedrooms to allow for expanding their tribe of homesteaders. They were even willing to overpay if it would ensure that the home would be the perfect catalyst to produce the experiences they most wanted to have.

A relatively short time after Derek and Anne moved into their small palace in St. Barts, things started to turn for the worse. Anne felt isolated on the island, and although she tried to make friends, she couldn't help but feel like an outsider. Before long she stopped leaving the house and dipped into a depression that Derek thought warranted antidepressant medication, though he couldn't get her to agree to see a doctor. Derek, too, felt alone. He would make trips back to the States to see friends, and once in a while his family would visit (they were very impressed with the house, as intended). The feeling of isolation crept into their relationship, and even though they still felt like they should be in their honeymoon period, the "spark" was dimming.

On advice from a professional relationship expert, they left St. Barts and found a modest rental house in Arizona near a few friends and family. The island mansion sat empty while Anne started to perk up, fueled by a more robust support system and more opportunities to engage in meaningful activities. A few months later, Derek sold the house on St. Barts (for an undisclosed loss) and now reports that their relationship has never been better. "It took some getting used to," Derek told Bryan. "The place in Arizona is certainly not as impressive as what we had in St. Barts. But we're so much happier here. Looking back, I can't believe we thought it was a good idea to go all the way out there [to a tropical island] all alone like that. It's a good reminder of what's really important."

Meanwhile, in San Rafael, the four couples are ecstatic, most of all Matt and Erica, and their home is becoming an important gathering place for their community. They all are helping one another in just about every important area of life, from parenting, to eating better, to clarifying and living more purposeful lives. Two of the men have even started a business partnership together.

What made the difference between the train wreck of the St. Barts home and the dream of the San Rafael community home? In the former case, the buyers were simply aiming to optimize one part of their lives—their experience of material wealth, through luxury living. Whereas in the San Rafael home, the buyers engaged in Systemic Spending, looking at how this expenditure/investment affected *every* area of their lives, from their sense of community, to their relationships and love lives, to their chance to work with people they love, to their ability to contribute with purpose. They spent systemically, so that their investment was aimed at maximizing not just financial wealth on a balance sheet, but their sense of wealth in all areas of their lives. They achieved much more happiness for the amount of money they spent, and thus they need to spend much less on other things to make themselves happy.

While this may seem like an extravagant example, the same principle always applies at any level of wealth or expenditure: the more you learn how to derive happiness from the money you spend—using the skills we have shared in this chapter—the less you will need to spend to be happy. And the more that will be left over for savings (a crucial part of the SAFE plan). And more money will also be left over for investing in your earning power, the topic to which we now turn.

CHAPTER 2

THE SUPER SKILLS:
The Most Valuable, Sought After, Rewarded, Compensated, and Universally Beneficial Human Skills

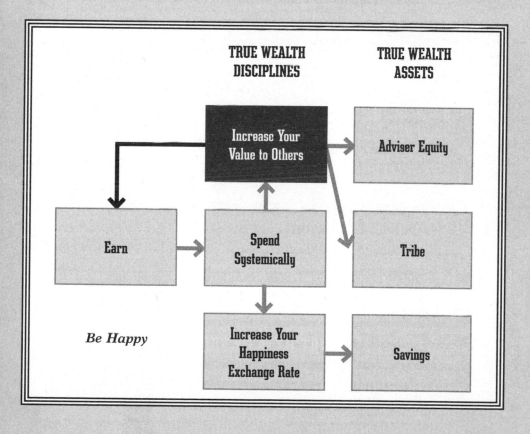

■ SYSTEMIC SKILL BUILDING ■

■ THE SUPER SKILLS ■

■ THE MARKET SKILLS ■

■ WHY LEVERAGED INCOME BEATS PASSIVE INCOME ■

"I'm open to leaving my job and starting a business," the soft-spoken, conservatively dressed young man said to Bryan across the lunch table. "But you have to understand where I've come from."

This man, Jesse Eichner, had a very unique and powerful skill, and Bryan knew that if he could encourage Jesse to leave his job and start a company, Jesse could convert that "Super Skill" into massive earning potential.

Bryan knew that Jesse was making $115,000 per year at his current job, and that he had never started a company before. Bryan thought to himself, "He's probably going to tell me he comes from a very conservative background and that even though he's in his late twenties, he still feels the need to justify his career choices to his parents. They are going to think he's *crazy* for leaving a sure thing and starting out on his own." Bryan has heard this story many times before, so he started to prepare his rebuttal: an explanation of how valuable Jesse is—because of his unique and powerful skill—and how Bryan could think of at least a dozen companies that would hire Jesse on the spot; so even if his new company was not successful, he was likely to end up in a more favorable financial position at a different company; that his parents would respect him more in the long run for taking risks and believing in himself; that he was just experiencing a little fear, and Bryan was happy to help him realize that it's actually safer for him to bet on himself than on anything else.

But then, Jesse said something that shocked Bryan.

"You see, just a few years ago, I was homeless."

"Say again?"

"I really came from nothing. I had no prospects. No job. No apartment. No skills. No way of earning money. Nothing. I can hardly believe that I make as much money as I do now, and I don't want to do anything to screw it up."

"Just a few years ago?" Bryan's admiration for him shot through the roof. "How did you learn to do what you do?"

"Books, mostly. And the Internet. I decided that I was willing to do anything to get out of my bad situation, so I tried to think of things that most companies need, but everyone hates to do. That's when I decided to learn how to do cold calling."

Cold calling is the process of calling on prospective customers with whom you have no relationship and who are not expecting you to call. As you can imagine, it's an exercise in repeated rejection and an invitation to be abruptly interrupted, hung up on, or even called names. Most people simply refuse to do it, even when it's the best way to improve a company's bottom line. When done well, it can be like financial magic. Start with nothing and make customers magically appear out of thin air.

Jesse had learned a few basic techniques from sales books. He then got a job working on commission only and was eager to show his new employer that he could be a valuable asset. He made about one hundred outbound calls every day. That's an average of one every six minutes. He was able to talk to an actual person, something Jesse calls "a connect," only one in ten times. He made about ten connects per day, and was able to get two to three of those ten to agree to meet with Jesse's boss, who would then sell the customer on the company's services.

"I just kept trying until I figured out how to get people to talk to me." At ten connects per day, Jesse explained, "I had lots of opportunities to try stuff. I tried everything. Once I figured out how to get at least some of the people to hear me out and actually consider what I had to offer, it got a lot easier. I brought in five million dollars in sales for my company last year, all on deals that came from me just sitting down and pounding the phone. Pretty crazy if you ask me."

Jesse's unique and powerful skill is that he can sit down in a room with nothing but a telephone and generate $5 million in deals, and he taught himself how to do it in less than three years. You can see why Bryan was so confident that his financial future was safe, and that the risk of leaving his current job for a few months to try something that would likely pay him several times his current salary was probably a risk worth taking. The only thing that seemed *crazy* to Bryan was that Jesse was getting paid only $115,000.

WHAT IS A SUPER SKILL?

We're not suggesting that every reader of this book should learn to do cold calling, nor is cold calling the only (or the easiest) way to increase your earning potential. Cold calling is, however, what we call a *Super Skill*: any skill that has a virtually guaranteed return on investment *regardless of your professional circumstances*. Super Skills increase your value to nearly every business, as well as the value of all your other skills.

Let's say you were a receptionist at a law firm, and you decided to invest one hundred hours in learning a new skill, and you were trying to choose between a Super Skill, like sales, and a typical professional skill, such as paralegal skills. As you'll see from this chart, learning the paralegal skills has a very direct and immediate benefit that sales skills don't. But when you take into account the fact that you don't know what you might want to do in the future, or what opportunities and obstacles might come your way during the span of your career, sales skills impact the entire system of your earning potential very differently from any typical skill.

The difference in lifetime return on your hundred-hour investment between the Super Skill and the typical skill is massive. It would most likely tally in the millions of dollars over the length of an entire career, but certainly hundreds of thousands. Add to the calculation the fact that paralegal skills are valuable only to law firms, while virtually all organizations value new customers, making your new sales skill marketable to companies in every industry, and you have effectively immunized yourself from the downside risk of fluctuations in the industry or general job market.

The core difference is that Super Skills have a positive

	SUPER SKILL (SALES)	TYPICAL SKILL (PARALEGAL)
Get paid for paralegal services	Not Helpful	Very Helpful
Get paid to do customer service	Somewhat Helpful*	Not Helpful
Get paid to get donations for firm's charity	Very Helpful	Not Helpful
Get paid to get support for internal projects	Very Helpful[†]	Not Helpful
Get paid to bring in new business	Very Helpful[‡]	Not Helpful
Get paid to recruit hard-to-get talent	Very Helpful	Not Helpful
Negotiating your raises and promotions	Very Helpful	Not Helpful
Finding a new job	Very Helpful[§]	Not Helpful
Getting into exclusive schools/programs	Very Helpful	Not Helpful
Starting your own business	Very Helpful	Not Helpful

---

* Sales is excellent preparation for the respect and patience required.
† Companies often need people to "sell" ideas internally to get budget approval.
‡ Imagine the bonus pay for a receptionist who lands a big new client.
§ Job interviews are essentially sales calls in which the product being sold is *you*.

systemic impact on all of your professional skills and, by extension, on your earning potential, regardless of your circumstances. In this regard, they are analogous to Systemic Spending, whereas typical skills are analogous to compartmentalized spending; typical skills benefit your earning potential only in your current professional context, and could be worthless in most other professional contexts.

You may not choose to get better at cold calling in particular, but it's not enough to just get better at a random skill and expect it to improve your financial situation. Consider not only which skills will increase your immediate income potential, but also which skills will systemically enhance the value other people get from your mix of personality traits, interests, and professional skills.

The four categories of Super Skills are *interpersonal, creative, technical,* and *physical.* These are the basic building blocks of delivering value to others. If you stop to consider what kinds of activities are most rewarding to you, what areas you get the most consistent positive feedback in, what kinds of tasks feel easy to you but hard to other people, and which Super Skills feel most natural to you, you can start to see which of the four categories might be the wisest investment for you.

Super Skills build on themselves, so the more developed you are in a particular area, the easier it will be for you to begin by further developing yourself in that same area. There is a finite list of Super Skills, and though you could argue that this is an incomplete list, any person who reaches even a modest level of competency at each of the following is so valuable to others, with such a strong earning potential, that his financial future is virtually guaranteed.

It's wise to consider developing *all* the key Super Skills over the course of your lifetime, but begin in the areas most exciting

INTERPERSONAL SKILLS	CREATIVE SKILLS	TECHNICAL SKILLS	PHYSICAL SKILLS
Leadership and Influence	Context Importing	Mental Models	Longevity
Public Speaking	Improvisation	Financial Models	Mental Focus
Visioning	Writing	Systems Thinking	Clean, Healthy Appearance
Teaching	Copywriting	Web Development	Clean and Organized Environment
Selling	Reading	Direct Marketing	Healthy Relationship with Alcohol/ Drugs
Networking and Building Tribe	Storytelling		Healthy Relationship with Your Sexuality
Holding Paradox	Design		

for you, so that each Super Skill you attain can help you master the next. Later on, we'll go into each of the Super Skills and how to invest in them in greater detail.

FORMULA FOR INVESTING IN YOUR EARNING POTENTIAL

The formula for investing in your income potential is first to choose a category of Super Skill that best fits your natural traits and interests and focus on a specific Super Skill that demands the least new behavior from you as possible, is valued the most by people whom you can easily meet, and enhances your earning potential across the greatest range of possible circumstances. Then find a credible education source (formal or informal) with a verified track record of students who have achieved positive results, put in the time and money required to excel, and make a commitment (such as joining a project at work) that requires you to put your new skill into practice in order to keep the commitment.

In Jesse's case, he chose the *interpersonal* category, focused on the Super Skill of *sales* (in the form of cold calling), found *books* and *blog posts* that were recommended by successful salespeople, studied the material in depth, and then took a *job* that required him to practice every day. He followed the formula perfectly, and the results were predictably great—with emphasis on the word "predictably." Once you've reached a reasonable degree of competence in your new Super Skill, repeat the process again.

> EARNING POTENTIAL =
> 1) CATEGORY OF SUPER SKILL
> 2) SPECIFIC SUPER SKILLS
> 3) EDUCATION SOURCE
> 4) COMMITMENT

MARKET SKILLS: RELATIVE RISKS AND REWARDS

Michael recently observed a sales conversation between a twenty-something Internet whiz kid, Neil Patel (founder of the analytics companies Crazy Egg and KISSmetrics), and a fifty-something founder and owner of a business that had been around longer than the kid had been alive.

The fifty-something was considering whether to buy an expensive marketing consulting package provided by the twenty-something.

Neil had a BA, but other than that had zero formal credentials in business or marketing. He had no MBA, no impressive list of Madison Avenue advertising agencies or Wall Street investment banks as past employers: in the formal credential department, no nothin'.

And yet, the older gentleman was listening attentively to what he had to say, and eventually did go on to sign a contract with Neil worth six figures.

Neil did not bring a lot of *traditional, formal* credibility to the table. And yet think of all the other forms of credibility Neil brought to the table:

- A track record of two successful multimillion-dollar businesses in the field.

- A highly regarded industry blog with well-written, lively, detailed posts on his area of expertise, which received dozens of comments and hundreds of tweets, likes, and shares per post.

- A Google PageRank on his blog coming in at a solid five, meaning that his content was deemed by Google to be relevant in his field.

- An impressive "About" page on that site, which narrated in detail his rags-to-riches story of rising from first-generation immigrant to serial entrepreneur with multiple successful businesses under his belt (with many ups and downs along the way).

- 117,000 Twitter followers (while he follows less than half as many) and 17,000 Facebook subscribers—he was clearly a celebrity in social media.

- 500-plus LinkedIn connections, including six glowing recommendations from clients.

- A large swath of the New York and San Francisco entrepreneurial community were his friends on Facebook—so
  he was clearly not a loner, but rather embedded in a vi-
  brant, relevant network of friends and connections.

Whether you're an employee, self-employed, or starting a
business that employs others, few things will affect your earning
power as strongly as your credibility with potential employers or
potential customers and clients. Less and less, such credibility
depends on formal credibility from degrees, awards, or affilia-
tions, or even a résumé list of what skills you've amassed. More
and more, credibility comes from the ability to produce results,
and to share and document those results in a verifiable way.

Neil's sales ability was certainly a factor in his six-figure
windfall that day, but it was the weight and power of his results-
based credibility that really made the difference. Impressive results come from focusing on a few highly marketable typical
skills, which we'll call "Market Skills," and wrapping them in
an array of Super Skills.

In Neil's case, he had invested heavily in the Market Skill of
Web analytics. There are lots of people who have invested in
this skill, and many who are undoubtedly more skilled than
Neil. But he combined this skill with the Super Skills of *writing* (his blog), *copywriting* (his persuasive writing that converts
Web visitors to customers), *sales* (what he was demonstrating in
this meeting), *scientific method* and *systems thinking* (which he
used to develop his methodology for achieving results), *storytelling* (which he used to help customers who don't understand
Web analytics to grasp the benefits of his services), and so on.
The Super Skills on their own would not have been enough,
but they served as a financial supercharger for Neil's chosen
Market Skill.

The Market Skills can be categorized under the same headings as the Super Skills: *interpersonal, creative, technical,* and *physical.* Unlike Super Skills, there are nearly infinite Market Skills within each category, with highly variable financial rewards and highly variable learning curves. You most likely have already invested a considerable amount in one or more Market Skills, and it may seem logical to simply continue charging forth reinvesting in the same set of Market Skills, but let's take a step back and look at Market Skills a little more strategically.

Like any investment, each Market Skill has a risk-to-reward ratio. Unlike with most other investments, though, this risk-to-reward ratio is known to you in advance and is relatively stable and predictable. From the perspective of financial returns, it's obviously riskier to invest in the Market Skill of singing in a rock band than to invest in the Market Skill of running a team of customer service professionals. It may not be obvious, though, if Web analytics or Web design is a better Market Skill investment. Or learning a foreign language versus learning to be a lab technician. To understand which Market Skills are going to have the greatest positive impact on your earning potential, you'll need to understand the possible risks and rewards at a more granular level.

Risk, in this case, is measured by how difficult it is to gain the minimum amount of the skill required to expect a decent wage. The variability of opportunity, degree of luck involved, average length of time it takes to learn, and reliance on special traits like high intelligence or high charisma are all part of difficulty. Reward is measured by the financial compensation and nonfinancial lifestyle benefits available to the *top 20 percent* of earners who trade on that skill, relative to the bottom 80 percent and to people in other trades. Nonfinancial benefits include things like status, fun, recognition, freedom, power, and access.

Based on this, different categories of Market Skills start to take on different risk/reward profiles. Physical Market Skills, such as the ability to operate a forklift, are relatively low risk, but also low reward. Operating a forklift, for example, is inexpensive to learn. It doesn't take a long time to reach minimum competency, and a large percentage of those who attempt to learn are able to do it. On the rewards side, it is relatively easy to find a job that pays a minimal living wage based on the Market Skill of operating a forklift, but the financial benefits of the top 20 percent of forklift operators in the world are not that great, and don't vary far beyond those of the bottom 80 percent. And the nonfinancial rewards are *very* limited; we've never seen a forklift operator get VIP treatment at a club merely because of his profession.

Contrast this with a creative Market Skill, such as oil painting, which is on the high-risk side. As with forklift operating, it's relatively inexpensive to learn. However, unlike with forklift operating, it is virtually impossible to find an entry-level oil-painting position, meaning that the vast majority of oil painters are unable to make a living wage from their Market Skill. There is a huge reward, however, for breaking through to the top.

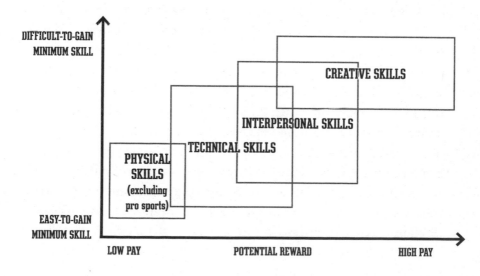

While these may seem like extreme examples, they point to a predictable risk/reward profile that can be generalized to the *category* of Market Skill, not just to the skill itself.

When looking at the marketability of skills, you'll see that physical skills tend to have the quickest and most reliable return on investment, but cap out at the lowest total reward. The easiest technical skills are a little more challenging to master, are in relatively high demand, and have a higher cap on earning potential. Those with the highest-paid technical skills, such as scientists and CTOs, earn an enviable wage, typically in the hundreds of thousands per year.

There's a fairly significant increase in potential reward for interpersonal skills, because the two top-paying jobs in most corporations are that of the CEO and the top-performing sales-person—jobs that rely on mastering Interpersonal Super Skills. The highest-paid interpersonal Market Skills command tens of millions per year. It can sometimes take a lot longer to learn how to lead teams or sell well enough to offer those skills as your core Market Skill, but entry-level managers often command higher salaries than entry-level technicians.

On the top end of both risk and reward are the creative skills. Highly successful actors, musicians, and painters (and even some writers) enjoy some of the greatest financial and non-financial rewards our socioeconomic system has to offer, but these fields are also the hardest to break into, and require the most investment in skill building before even the smallest amount of financial compensation is warranted. Commercial applications of creativity, such as graphic design, product design, and creating advertising jingles, have a risk/reward profile similar to technical skills at the lower end (including a greater reliance on technique than on creativity), but can have higher risk and higher rewards than technical skills at the top. (Also, we should point out that certain physical Market Skills, such as attempting to make it as a professional athlete, or a runway model, have a risk/reward profile closer to that of rock musicians than of construction workers.)

Based on the risk/reward profiles we've discussed, we would recommend focusing primarily on either an interpersonal Market Skill or a technical Market Skill for the majority of readers. At their core, interpersonal skills are about inspiring and influencing others. Technical skills are about understanding the truth of a given system or situation, which often requires periods of solitary thinking work. Choose the kind of work that's best for you. If you are a passionate artist and you can't stand the thought of giving up your dream profession, continue to invest in your ability to refine and improve your art, and over time, if you combine your creative skill with enough interpersonal skills such as networking, copywriting, and sales, you will be more likely to earn a healthy salary while doing what you love most.

Much of the long-term, top-level success in creative skills depends on luck. Realize that your early success will come almost entirely from your Super Skills and not from your artistic talent, and any greater success in the long term will be the result of the alchemy between your investment in improving your artistic craft and the (often unpredictable) tastes and preferences of your audience.

If you invest $5,000 to $10,000 in developing your Market Skill and one or two additional Super Skills each year, you will continually be upgrading your value to others—provided you invest in education sources that effectively teach you these skills. If you supercharge your Market Skills with regular investment in Super Skills, it would be reasonable to predict hundreds of thousands of dollars in returns in the first five years, and millions of dollars of returns over a much greater period of time—either in raises, promotions, and salaried positions, or in your ability to start your own company. It's the most recession-proof, bubble-proof, bad-decade-proof, layoff-proof investment strategy in existence. Even if the entire world economy collapses due to China's inability to keep buying American debt, as some extreme futurists warn, *being seen as valuable to other people* and having skills that bring value to others will still be relevant. Even if we stop valuing money, we will always value value itself.

PASSIVE INCOME VS. LEVERAGED INCOME

Yes, you do have to actually work to realize financial gains from the practice of being valuable to others. That means letting go (for now) of the dream of so-called passive income—living high off the hog from financial investments that supposedly grow without any work on your part. But *working* doesn't mean that you are stuck on some treadmill to nowhere, as many investment books would have you believe.

What makes passive income attractive is the value of freedom of choice. Passive income means you get to choose what you do with your time, where you live, when you go to the beach, and how late you sleep in. While we want you to give up on your dream of passive income, we don't want you to let go of your value of freedom. In fact, we want you to express it even more fully.

When you leverage your income by investing in your value to others, you can gain the same freedom of choice that successful passive investors have, by being so valuable in a work context that you can have your pick of projects, positions, teams, companies, and industries. Once they reach a certain degree of mastery in their Market and Super Skills, the most valuable members of business teams can often determine their own hours, location, and working conditions. Not to mention that these same skills afford you the option to start your own companies if you wish.

If you are lucky enough to achieve it, passive income may offer you the choice of playing Xbox all day, but it rarely gives you the opportunity to sit on the board of the nonprofits that inspire you most, have dinner with your living heroes like Sir Richard Branson or your favorite musicians, or be invited to be the keynote speaker at a cutting-edge conference in your field of choice. You are free to choose any of these options if you've earned them through your own power of contribution and value to others. Many of our close friends and colleagues have these kinds of experiences on a regular basis. Not because they were born with extraordinary gifts or advantages (many came from extremely humble beginnings) but because they have spent a decade or more consistently investing in themselves.

The same cannot be said for those who have spent a decade trying to crack the code of passive income. In our experience, the skill of generating passive income has a similar risk/reward profile as that of trying to be a movie star—and leaves most of its suitors broke and disenchanted, as most aspiring movie stars are (but without the creative fulfillment or romanticism that comes from being a starving artist).

We believe that, for the vast majority of readers, investing in active earning potential requires less knowledge, less risk, and results in more gains than investing in passive income.

Just how much can you gain? The career ladder leads, at the peak, to being CEO (and being an entrepreneur is, in some ways, a parallel, shortcut path to becoming CEO of a company). Thus, while not everyone wants to be CEO or an entrepreneur, the earnings difference between being an average employee versus being a CEO roughly delimits the scale that everyone on the career ladder is between, with those on the higher rungs earning significantly more for each step up. In a typical U.S. company, CEOs—who represent the pinnacle of investment in the interpersonal skill of leadership—get paid 380 times the salary of the average worker in the same firm. According to a Spencer Stuart study of CEOs in 2004, the average CEO spends about thirty years in the workforce, investing in her leadership, before getting the top job.[1] We'd like to see an investment salesperson try to match that performance benchmark—38,000 percent over three decades. It's even more when you consider that every CEO probably was paid a lot less than the average current worker when she started. We would hardly describe 108 percent compound annual growth as running in some kind of circular rat race, "trading dollars for hours," etc.

Of course we can't guarantee that you'll be a CEO one day. And you may not aspire to anything of the kind. But we can (and do) argue that self-investments in Super Skills, such as those required to be a CEO, are far more predictable, known, and readily available to every reader of this book than the factors leading to success in any passive investment class. Even if you never become a CEO, learning the skills you would need to have in order to be one will guide your self-investments in the right direction toward significant career and earnings advancement.

CHAPTER 3

INVEST IN INTERPERSONAL SUPER SKILLS

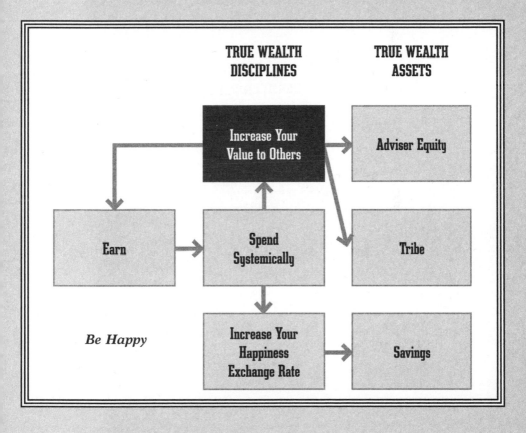

- LEADERSHIP AND INFLUENCE -
- PUBLIC SPEAKING -
- VISIONING -
- TEACHING -
- SELLING -
- NETWORKING AND BUILDING TRIBE -
- HOLDING PARADOX -

Raj Bandyopadhyay had a problem.

His dream career was to work in the burgeoning field of data science. Understandable, as it's one of the hottest sectors in the job market. He was an experienced software engineer—so it's not as though he were coming to the problem as a line cook or a cashier. But in Atlanta, where he lived, there were thousands of software engineers wanting to get into the field who had a lot more specialized Market Skills and experience than he did.

So how did he, just a year later, get recommended to the CEO of Pindrop Security, one of the hottest start-ups in Atlanta—it had just received $12 million in funding from Andreessen Horowitz—as a great candidate to build the company's brand-new data science team from scratch? Why did the start-up aggressively recruit Raj over a period of two weeks until he finally accepted what was his first "C-level" job and the highest-ranking position in the field, chief data scientist?

He knew that most jobs are awarded by referral—up to 80 percent by some accounts—so he figured he would make some initial contacts at networking events. He searched Meetup.com for meetups on data science in his hometown of Atlanta. There were meetups for users of particular software tools within the field, but no general meetups for the entire field of data science in Atlanta. Dead end.

Around this time, Raj heard an interview Michael did for personal finance author Ramit Sethi, about connecting with powerful and influential people, in which Michael gave the following piece of advice: "The best way to meet people at networking events is to *host* the networking event."

Raj was a software engineer, not an event producer. He didn't know anyone who would come to a networking event that he hosted, and he didn't know enough about the field to develop a compelling presentation to draw people he didn't know to attend. But the advice wouldn't leave his brain. What if, instead of a dead end, the fact that there weren't any data science meetups in Atlanta was his big opportunity?

"I contacted Dr. Nikolaos Vasiloglou, one of the most respected experts in machine learning [an aspect of data science] in Atlanta," Raj says, "and I asked, 'If I can get a room full of people interested in your work together on a weeknight to listen to you, will you give a talk for us?'"

Vasiloglou agreed, becoming the event's major draw. With that agreement in place, Raj and his friend Travis Turney started Data Science ATL (www.meetup.com/Data-Science-ATL). They invited every tech person they knew or vaguely knew in the city, and based on their strong first speaker, they got an initial crowd of thirty people, "which is considered pretty good for a first tech-based meetup," Raj said.

Since then, Raj and Travis have organized almost one talk per week, inviting different experts in the field. The quality of the events and the new outlet for people to talk about a shared interest served as the group's marketing, and word of the group spread through the Atlanta tech scene. During this same time period, Raj was reading books and taking online courses, so he could contribute more and more to the discussion at every meetup.

They started having fifty people show up for their events, then a hundred, and even two hundred for a recent meetup. Over time, Raj felt less like an outsider and more like a ringleader in the Atlanta data science community. Because of his leadership in this community, he was recommended for the leadership position at Pindrop.

Raj's story illustrates the power of Interpersonal Super Skills.

As his experience shows, it is arguably the best potential bang for your time and money investment buck, vaulting you past those who focus on just Market Skills—like being a good data scientist. In this chapter, we break down the key skills for you.

INTERPERSONAL SUPER SKILLS APPLIED:
THE ESSENTIAL SKILLS OF A BUSINESS INFLUENCER

Being an influential person has very little to do with enrolling people in your personal agenda. It's much more about understanding the motivations of each key individual or group within a system. Then detecting the agenda that furthers those motivations, serves the greatest purpose, and aligns with your values and objectives; and finally enrolling *yourself* in that larger agenda. This is one way to ensure that your investment in your own influence doesn't degrade to a study in deception and manipulation.

With this perspective, investing in the building blocks of influence, the key Interpersonal Super Skills—which we define as leadership, public speaking, visioning, teaching, sales skills, networking, and tribe building, all of which we discuss in more detail below—will improve your ability to perceive and wield the powers that fuel decision making.

Leadership and Influence

Forget any associations you have between *leadership* and neighboring ideas of authority, being in charge, being charismatic, or getting to tell people what to do. These concepts are not helpful in guiding you to invest in your leadership. You can lead a group from any position, with any title. At its core, leadership is about moving people's hearts and minds from point A to point B. If you change a person's heart and mind, you change what they want, and their behavior naturally follows. This is raw leadership, and it's the single most sought-after skill when wooing executives to take the highest-paid salaried positions: leadership positions.

To start using the Interpersonal Super Skill of leadership, understand why people are choosing point A. Then identify in them a motivation consistent with point B, and find a way to communicate the connection between their already-present motivation and your point B. If you want to encourage a team of volunteers to work longer hours, find out *why* they became volunteers in the first place and give them the opportunity to have more of whatever that is by putting in more effort.

This communication is primarily accomplished through your commitment, authenticity, and clarity. It is as much a matter of *being* as *doing*. The reason "leading by example" is so effective is that it demonstrates this commitment. If you are not willing to work longer, then your story about how working longer is going to be beneficial for others starts to smell fishy. If you don't really believe working longer will be beneficial to them, again it will smell fishy. This is probably why honesty was found to be the most important quality that people want in a leader, according to research done by James M. Kouzes and Barry Z. Posner for their book *The Leadership Challenge.* Leadership, as it turns out, has very little to do with charisma, being an extrovert, or being a people person. It has much more to do with combining honest empathy for other people (point A) with a vision of a collective future you authentically believe in (point B).

This suggests that the only limit to the leadership and influence you could develop, provided you invest enthusiastically, is your emotional connection with those you wish to lead and your own true belief in the existence of a collective future point B that furthers each person's deeper motivations and desires.

Two trends are making leadership and influence competence even more treasured by companies. First, "command and control"-style leadership typical of big industrial-era manufacturing firms is phasing out as the knowledge economy becomes the driver of growth. People, especially the younger generations entering the workforce, no longer assume that those with authority also know best. Therefore the cost of bad leadership (for example, just telling people what they should do and expecting them to do it) is growing inside corporations. Second, as our economy becomes more and more globalized and the number of people who can easily interact through technology exponentially rises, the need for companies and organizations to coordinate the collaborative effort of many people behind a single objective is also rising exponentially.

In the 1990s, conventional wisdom held that the ideal number of people directly reporting to a manager was eight. Any more and it was thought that the manager wouldn't have enough time and attention to guide and direct each person. As company structures move away from the "command and control" model of leadership and get more autonomous, leaders in business find themselves with much flatter organizations with many more direct reports. At Google—one of the most profitable companies in the world—some business leaders have had more than eight hundred people reporting to them directly. This means that leaders at Google must be one hundred times more efficient in their ability to lead and influence.

Start now. Practice influencing people to create a better future, whether with your customers, your friends, or your coworkers. Call your shots. Have a specific future in mind, enroll them in the vision of that future, and start matching their desires to your desired outcomes. Measure your leadership by how enthusiastic and successful your followers are at creating your envisioned result. Invest in reputable leadership teachers, authors, and coaches and vigorously apply what you learn. We suggest many examples throughout the rest of this chapter, and mention resources in our "Reading" section in chapter 4. This one Super Skill could be the single most valuable "sure thing" in investment history.

Public Speaking

Great investors look for valuable assets that other people aren't likely to buy. A relatively small investment in one of these undervalued assets can yield fantastic returns because the lack of competition creates an artificially low barrier to entry and therefore a much greater return. Perhaps the most undervalued Super Skill is public speaking. You need only sit in on a few typical corporate presentations to see how rare this form of self-investment is. For leaders and influencers, however, an inability to communicate a compelling message to a group can be the equivalent of career death. Even if you never imagine yourself using public gatherings as a means of gaining credibility or demanding the $2,000 to $50,000 in fees that professional public speakers are often paid, you are still working in a knowledge economy. You are trading knowledge with those around you to promote your ideas and motivate actions. And the most powerful venue for this exchange is still an in-person meeting.

Investing in public speaking doesn't have to start with a high price tag. For $56 you can join Toastmasters International, a communication and leadership development community that emphasizes public speaking. Once you join, you attend meetings, give short speeches, and trade valuable feedback for improvement. Members report that their Toastmasters experiences have helped them write and publish books, get leadership positions, and even get TV and radio appearances.

Visioning

If influence is leading people from point A to point B, the Super Skill of *visioning* is applying clarity to point B. Leaders spend time clarifying for themselves the future that they want to create, including how each person involved fits into that future. In leadership training courses that Bryan co-leads with his wife, Jennifer Russell, she explains, "If you are having trouble getting people to follow you, it's probably because they can't see clearly where you are leading them. Great leaders paint a picture of the future so vivid, you can imagine it like a painting in a picture frame set on the path where you currently are. If your vision is detailed enough and clear enough, others will feel they can almost step *through* the frame and onto the path in the picture. When the future you paint feels as real to people as the present moment, they effortlessly follow you and help you create that future."

How do you gain this clarity of vision? We find that the key to unlocking your own Super Skill of *visioning* comes from a very unlikely source. We are in a culture that devalues negative judgments about other people and things, labeling them "judgmental." Conventional wisdom advises you not to even mention anything you find wrong with a situation in a professional context unless you also have a suggestion for fixing it. This advice points to the interpersonal cost of voicing a negative judgment. People don't like negativity, especially if it exposes a potential weakness or an embarrassing oversight of theirs. But judgments themselves are potentially very valuable. If you were to list all of your negative judgments about a situation and evaluate them, you would begin to see more clearly what you want to create by eliminating everything that it's not. If you don't like people who talk too much, perhaps you have a vision of an environment that values more listening. If you don't like people who waste your time, perhaps you value more efficiency. Trace your judgments to discover your values, and paint a clear picture of the future that expresses those values fully.

For a vision to be clear, it must also be clear to *other people*, specifically the intended followers. That means that visioning, just like the other Interpersonal Super Skills, is a two-way street. It involves communicating your vision, and also understanding which parts are clear and believable to your audience and which parts need work. One of the most common complaints about poor leadership in a business setting is that the vision isn't clear enough. Without a clear vision, employees don't feel confident in making their own decisions, and productivity suffers.

New leaders often think that *visioning* is located in their own minds, and therefore if it is clear to them, it must be clear enough. The vision that matters, however, is the collective vision in the minds of those you hope to lead. An experienced leader invests in her ability to detect and correct any variances between the clear vision in her own mind and the vision in the minds of the people. When the collective vision is clear, then each person is free to employ creativity and make decisions that all independently support the same positive outcome.

Notice the ways that you are pleased or not pleased with your current environment. Every time you're not pleased with it, it's because you have somewhere in your mind an alternative future that it could be. Instead of just expressing your displeasure at the current state, the more you understand what reference point you're using that makes you *feel* that displeasure (i.e., your vision of the possible future) and can see it clearly and articulate it and describe it to people, the more you're practicing the skill of visioning. It is the inner work of developing the reference

—

point, the ability to articulate that vision, plus the outer work of listening to determine if others see how clear your vision truly is.

Teaching

Another specialized form of influence, *teaching* is the art of leading people to a point B in which they are more educated and capable. It is absolutely essential to a successful SAFE plan, because it provides leverage. If you know how to sell, you'll make money. If you know how to teach someone else to sell, you'll make money, friends, and the potential to make money and equity from the sales efforts of other people as well.

Web sites like Learni.st, Udemy.com, Clarity.fm, and Skillshare.com all provide ordinary people with the opportunity to teach something online. You can test and optimize your own teaching methods offline. Find friends or family members who want to learn how to do something you do well. Agree to teach them. Try different methods of teaching (more hands-on, more hands-off, letting them fail, correcting their mistakes, etc.) and test how effective each one is at bringing your student closer to your own level of competence in that area.

An ongoing investment in your teaching ability will soon make you a more valuable member of any team or company, because any skill you learn can then be multiplied throughout the organization.

Selling

You may never be in a position of formally selling something to a customer. Maybe you're an engineer, a scientist, or a mid-level manager within a large organization. But improving your sales skills and personal influence is still likely to be your most lucrative self-investment. Why?

Even if you are not selling a product for money in your own role, you are continually in an environment where ideas and projects are competing for limited resources. Sales skills are the most predictable way to increase your earnings over the long run. These skills add leverage to your already-existing technical skills (i.e., what you do for a living), because no matter how good you are at those skills, you won't get paid top dollar for them unless you convince others that your skills are *worth* top dollar.

The art of selling is the art of persuading others to commit their resources to your idea, product, or project. If you are able to garner support, you are a vastly more valuable member of the team. Every nonprofit needs fund-raisers. Every company needs customers. Every project needs internal funding. Every entrepreneur needs partners. Every investment needs investors. Every movement needs support. Selling is often the tipping point between an idea becoming reality or fading away into memory.

One resistance a lot of people have—and Michael used to have—to learning sales or persuasion is that it can sound manipulative. But competency in sales is not about changing someone else's mind in order to get them to buy. It isn't about getting someone to do something that they don't want to do. It's about discovering what path they already want to be on, and figuring out together if your product, idea, or course of action serves them along that path or not. It's an act of co-created discovery, which feels great to participate in.

What works are two things: asking what the person you are trying to sell to *cares about*, and then *caring about* the answers they give. The more the person you are trying to sell to talks about what they care about, the more likely you are to sell, because you are now in a better position to give them what they *actually* want, not what you *think* they want.

SPIN Selling, a fantastic research-based book by Neil Rackham, Jay Abraham's work on "consultative selling," and Bryan's own "Natural Selling System" course are all based on this basic understanding of how to create sustainable, loyal customers and leave everyone involved with a positive experience. Find a teacher who resonates with you and then buy his or her coursework and practice.

People who do not learn about sales tend to feel highly victimized by "the economy" as a nebulous force they don't understand. Anytime you find yourself blaming an outside force, such as the economy, it should serve as a signal that it's time to invest more in Interpersonal Super Skills. "The economy" doesn't create economic opportunity on an individual scale. People do. Specifically, people who are rainmakers—that is, those who have learned how to sell well. If you're feeling insecure in your career, or if you feel as though you may be switching your work sometime soon (either voluntarily or involuntarily), consider investing in learning how to become a rainmaker.

Networking and Tribe Building

Like sales, *networking* is emotionally and financially rewarding for those who understand it and an unpleasant or even repulsive chore for those who don't. Networking is essentially building a social circle, which takes time and can cost money but could be the best investment of your time and money in existence. Nearly everything we value in our lives—from our closest friends, to Michael's literary agent, to Bryan's record contract for the electronic music he produces (under the name NIMITAE), to tens of millions of dollars of business opportunities through the years for Bryan—has come through off-line, face-to-face social networking. The returns you can get via this kind of investing—both on a professional level and on a personal one—far surpass anything available to the average investor through investing in markets, and even surpass what's available from the other Super Skills, taken in isolation. Though networking is the key to building your tribe, an essential True Wealth asset, for now we will focus on the Interpersonal Super Skill of networking as a way to increase your value to others and maximize your earning potential.

If *selling* is about finding the match between what people want and what you have to offer, *networking* is finding the match between what people value and what they have to offer one another. If you think of your network as a hub and spokes, with the objective of creating as many connections to yourself (the hub) as possible, you are likely in for a lot of frustrating and unproductive evenings at awkward parties and stilted networking events. If you think of networking as building a tribe of people who share the same values and are excited to offer value to one another, then you are set up to utilize the power of tribe and become an influential community leader. (We share exactly *how* to go from the periphery of a few social circles to the center of a powerful entrepreneurial ecosystem or tribe in chapter 8, which focuses exclusively on tribe.)

Holding Paradox

There is one more Interpersonal Super Skill we need to talk about, though this one is perhaps more counterintuitive. There's something unique that every truly great leader does that the ones who aren't so great do not do. It has to do with their relationship to paradox.

Consider the common example of a leader who needs to convince her followers that, while the team is experiencing significant challenges and there is a very real risk of failure, ultimately the team will prevail. There are two ways a lesser leader could falter in this moment. The first is to simply pander to negativism: agreeing with everyone's feeling that the current situation is rough or hopeless, without offering any vision, possibility, or credible plan. This would be a good display of empathy, but it won't lead anyone to change. The second mistake would be to hold the opposite view, that the future is bright and the current setbacks are illusory or insignificant. This could be seen superficially as inspiring, but more likely it will backfire because it will be dismissed as being noncredible and unrelatable to the lived reality of the employees.

A superior leader learns how to hold paradox: to believe, at the same time, that the situation is dire and hopeful, meeting employees where they're at, but also convincing them of the actions they can take that will lead to a brighter future. The evidence is that things are bad (anyone denying this will be seen as a Pollyanna); and also, the evidence is that things are good (anyone denying this would be seen as a weak leader, lacking creativity to produce a positive way forward). Followers need to feel met in the reality that they are scared, yet they also need to be given a realistic expectation of future success.

When you're confronted with a paradox, you are presented with a choice. You can either ignore it and take a side (believe one side of the statement is true while the other is false), or you can do what we call *hold paradox*, which is to believe both contradictory statements or implications simultaneously. It's an expression of faith in a greater truth that is currently invisible to you, but resolves the paradox and allows for the truth of both sides to harmoniously coexist. This is what great leaders do.

Holding paradox is the ability to literally hold in your mind the truth and acknowledge, for example, your utter insignificance on a cosmic scale, and then without allowing that experience to dissipate, add to it the unmistakable truth of your profound significance to those you love.

A leader who chooses sides in a paradox will find that there are people who cannot follow him or her because an important underlying belief doesn't feel represented in the leader. As an example, would you follow a leader who believed the future was absolutely certain, with no variability? But would you follow anyone who had no idea whatsoever what the future held? Not likely. You would probably feel inspired to follow a leader who could hold the paradox of certainty about the future: absolute clarity of vision without doubting that there are vast terrains yet unknown about the future. Any denial of one half of a paradox causes you to lose the connection to those who believe in that part more fully.

Leaders who hold paradox are standing in the intersection between the two seemingly contradictory truths and finding a center ground where a much deeper understanding arises. When you sense paradox, you've found a key to a dimensional doorway. Unlock the door (by holding the paradox) and your consciousness will expand to include all the perspectives, benefits, and insights offered native to the new dimensionality. Almost like a zipper, holding together two folds of the universe, just waiting for you to unzip your current reality and reconsider *everything* based on a new context.

Suppose that you are only two-dimensional, and that you've never seen, experienced, or even considered 3-D objects or the 3-D space in which they live.

Now suppose that you encountered the following apparent paradox:

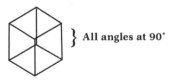 } **All angles at 90°**

How could it be? It makes no sense. The object *clearly* is not solely made up of right angles. Is it a lie? Is it a trick? Your peers take sides. Some decide the picture was drawn in error. Some decide that the error lies in the text. You decide to hold the paradox.

If you see the image as a crisscross of lines at odd angles, you can easily see it in two dimensions because you are *thinking in two dimensions*. As you look at the object, force your imagination to "make" the angles 90 degrees, or exactly perpendicular. Suddenly the image "jumps off" the page and becomes a cube in your consciousness, because you've shifted to *thinking in three dimensions*. Now that you have expanded your consciousness to include additional dimensionality, there is no paradox. There is only an ordinary cube, accompanied by a mundane observation—a "stating of the obvious."

What's more, your new three-dimensional insight isn't limited to this image of a cube, but instantly reframes, or recontextualizes, *everything*, past, present, and future. Notice that the paradox only exists when an object (or idea or phenomenon) is witnessed through the lens of *less dimensionality* that is native to it: 3-D objects viewed in 2-D space, etc. Let this serve as a reminder to you that there is a broader way of thinking available every time you sense a contradiction or paradox.

This is the power of paradox, and this is why we call holding paradox a dimensional gateway. Life is littered with these little clues, where the seams of our limited sense of reality don't quite line up and are just waiting for us to evolve our thinking. Every time you experience a paradox or conflict between truths, know that there is a new understanding waiting for you to behold—as fundamental as waking up to three dimensions after having lived only in two.

Through intellectual honesty, you can start to hold these paradoxes, unlocking dimensions of consciousness among apparent dichotomies such as the masculine versus feminine, the material versus spiritual dimensions, the agentic (identification with self as an "agent" acting on the world) versus the communal (identification with others as a "we," acting on all selves), and countless more.

Perhaps the most important leadership paradox is about change itself. To grossly generalize, Eastern wisdom teaches us that the present moment is perfect, without any alteration or adjustment. In this conception, "enlightenment" is achieved by the full realization of the perfection of the now moment. Western wisdom teaches us that the ultimate human expression is that of progress and evolution; that "a better tomorrow" deserves all of our attention. You have the potential to harness these two powerful opposing truths and gain the power of this apparent paradox but also the potential to lose the ability to lead those who are inculcated in one or the other culture.

Any leader who can fully acknowledge the perfection of the present moment and fully endorse our evolutionary drive to grow and change can unleash inspiration and motivation among followers on both sides of the paradox.

CHAPTER 4

INVEST IN CREATIVE SUPER SKILLS

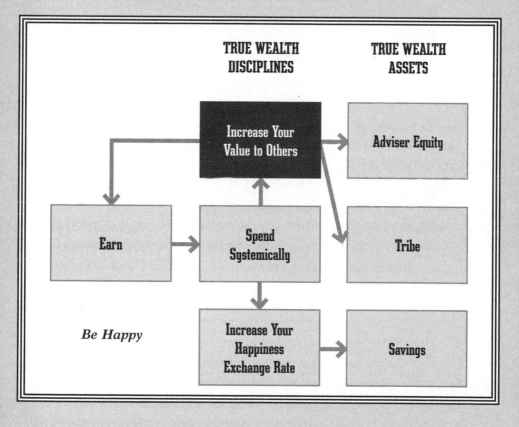

■ CONTEXTUAL IMPORTING ■

■ IMPROVISATION ■

■ WRITING, COPYWRITING, READING ■

■ STORYTELLING ■

■ DESIGN ■

The most valuable urinal the world has ever known was created in New York City in 1917.

It had no diamonds in it, nor any precious stones at all. It was not made of gold or platinum, but of porcelain, just like every other urinal. In fact, in every respect, it *was* just like every other urinal, into which the common men of the time were relieving themselves in public bathrooms around the world.

In 1917, an artist calling himself R. Mutt signed his name to such a urinal—said to be a Bedfordshire model bought at a foundry showroom on Fifth Avenue—and submitted it to an exhibition organized by the Society of Independent Artists, paying their $6 fee. Even though it was a nonjuried exhibit, open to anyone who paid the fee, the Society's board took the extraordinary step of exercising jury powers. They turned down Mr. Mutt's submission as not being art and returned the urinal to him with a rejection slip.

A photograph of the urinal—the only remaining record of the original—appeared in an obscure art journal called *The Blind Man*, along with an editorial denouncing the board's decision. "Whether Mr. Mutt with his own hands made the fountain or not has no importance. He CHOSE it. He took an ordinary article of life, placed it so that its useful significance disappeared under a new title and point of view—created a new thought for that object."[1]

Mr. Mutt, it turned out, was a young artist named Marcel Duchamp, associated with an emerging avant-garde art movement called Dada. *The Fountain*, as the work was titled, took on a life of its own. The original was lost, but over the years

Duchamp authorized fifteen replicas, one of which is now held in the permanent collection of the Pompidou Centre in Paris, another in the Tate Modern in London.

In 2004, in a survey of five hundred British art experts, *The Fountain* was voted the most influential piece of modern artwork.[2] Think about that for a moment. Modern art includes masterworks such as Picasso's *Les Demoiselles d'Avignon* and *Guernica*, Dalí's *The Persistence of Memory*, the work of Kandinsky and Matisse, and on and on, and the most influential work is . . . a manufactured pisser with a signature on it?

"[W]ith this single 'readymade' work," one commentator wrote, "Duchamp invented conceptual art and severed for ever the traditional link between the artist's labour and the merit of the work."[3]

(It took forty-four years for this line of thinking to move the entire way down the digestive tract of modern art, to its final, scatological end point. In 1961, Italian artist Piero Manzoni tinned ninety cans with thirty grams each of his own excrement, labeling the cans "Artist's Shit." He originally sold the cans to the art market for their equivalent weight in gold—an obvious reference to the artist's ability to alchemize common objects into great value. Over time, however, the tins far outpaced the price of gold. In 2007, one of these ninety cans sold at a Sotheby's auction for around $160,000.[4] Later, there came to be some question as to whether the tins might actually contain mere plaster. No one was willing to take the $160,000 hit to ruin one of the pieces, open the tin and find out for sure. However, the mere suspicion of plaster, rather than genuine artist's dung as labeled, apparently made the value of the tins go down substantially.[5])

The authorized replicas of Duchamp's original are now worth as much as $3.6 million each.[6] Because it was lost, we'll never know the financial value of the original. But given the nine-figure valuations that other influential works at the top of that survey have fetched at auction, if the original were around today, it would certainly be worth eight figures, if not nine.

Before Duchamp got his hands on it, that urinal was worth whatever he paid for it at the store—probably a few hundred dollars at most, in today's dollars. But by seeing it outside of the context of "things to pee in," and instead within the context of modern art—a place where people with money are always looking for fresh, innovative, and scandalous ideas—he created millions of dollars in new value, not to mention influencing generations of artists to come. As the *Blind Man* article said, he "created a new thought for that object."

You might see this story as simply an example of the absurdity of the spending patterns of the super-rich, or as a parody of the greed and arbitrary tastes of art speculators, but there's an even more useful meaning here. Value depends on context. It is not a fixed, discrete attribute of an object—like color, size, or shape. Thus, you can often increase the value of something (or some skill set) simply by importing it into a different context. One of six Creative Super Skills, *contextual importing* is responsible for some of the most valuable art, inventions, discoveries, and innovations in history. In some ways it's like creativity's mother, giving birth to a flood of new thoughts and ideas.

THE LAST HUMAN SKILL

After influence, one of the most marketable attributes in the world is creativity, as expressed through the Creative Super Skills discussed in this chapter. The corporatized word for creativity is *innovation*, which can be thought of as creativity constrained by whatever operational goals the organization has. Innovation has made its way into the top values, initiatives, and areas of investment for most companies. Some believe that companies that fail to innovate are doomed to die.

Companies like Nike, Google, Zappos, Facebook, and Apple spend millions of dollars each year on new ways to foster and reward the creativity and innovation of their employees. It is widely understood that any tasks that rely primarily on algorithmic, procedural, or analytic intelligence are currently being either offshored to technically educated labor forces in the third world, or simply automated by computers and even robots.[7] This means that the spoils in the first world go to those whose skills simply cannot be automated. Some believe that robotic automation and artificial intelligence will one day be responsible for accomplishing nearly every labor task on Earth, leaving one last skill to the humans: creativity. Whether or not you believe this prophecy, it does suggest an often-overlooked relationship between creativity and job security.

Through the years, Bryan has been in hundreds of meetings called for the purpose of determining which employees to lay off and which to "save" during an unfortunate period of profit shrinking. The biggest influencers—and the most secure in their positions—tend to be the people in the meeting doing the deliberations. The conversation usually goes something like this:

> "Well, obviously we have to keep Mary [. . . because she's a huge influencer]."
> "Yes. And Stacey and James [. . . because they're salespeople who close big deals]."
> "How about marketing? Who can we spare there?"
> "Well, I *need* Alfonso. He's so creative."
> "Then I guess we'll lay off Susan or Jeff?"
> "Yes. Either one is fine."

Obviously, you'd rather be Alfonso than Susan or Jeff. But Susan and Jeff had a choice. They could have invested in their own creativity over the past months or years, and changed their fate. Just as most people think influence is a trait natural leaders are simply born with, you might think that your own creativity is fixed, and there's nothing you can do to expand it. But, in fact, there's a lot you can do to increase your own creativity and apply it more effectively to your work.

In the nature-versus-nurture debate, one thing is clear to both sides: some people *seem* to have a natural talent for creativity. And some people do not. The career-limiting error that most people make is to assume that the difference in "natural" talent dictates the difference in creative *value* that a person can offer. Creative value comes from applying your creativity, not merely from being born with talent.

For someone who doesn't apply their creativity to their work anyway, a big increase in creativity will have a very small effect on actual creative *value*. But if you bring 100 percent of your available creativity to what you do, then even a small increase in your creative capacity can convey a large benefit to your creative value. This is how a person with less natural talent can routinely produce more creative work than seemingly more talented peers, and this is why you should invest in your capacity to bring your creativity to your work, regardless of how you rate yourself in terms of "natural" talent.

THE TWO BIGGEST PITFALLS WHEN INVESTING IN YOUR CREATIVITY

The first pitfall to avoid while investing in your Creative Super Skills is believing that creativity is the same thing as learning the technique of any particular means of expression. You could learn violin or piano or ballroom dance or figure drawing—and millions of young people do—in a manner that is entirely rote and uncreative. Creativity requires that you bring some aspect of your *self* to your creation. You could learn to play songs in a technically accurate manner, without putting any of your *self* into it. While you would have learned a means of executing an artistic form, that doesn't mean you would have learned how to *express* yourself using that means.

Kira Roessler, a punk rock bassist (and former star sound editor for Bryan's first company, Franklin Media), referred to technical expertise, disparagingly, as "neck math." Meaning, guitarists would execute mathematically dizzying note sequences on the guitar *neck*, but without any feeling or meaning. This might be called the pitfall of "focusing too much on technique."

The second pitfall is the opposite—the belief that creativity is some unbridled expression of impulses, captured in media, like an emotional hissy fit in paint. Just slap some words together and you have a creative poem! Just throw some paint at a piece of paper (or on the wall!) and you have a creative painting! Just do the opposite of what's expected and you have innovation! This is the creativity of "everyone gets a gold star" in kindergarten art classes, and of certain executive "creativity workshops." It is based on the misconception that simply because the idea came from your mind or it was your hand holding the brush, that qualifies as putting your *self* into your creation. This pitfall might be called "focusing not enough on technique." You have to know the dimensions of a face if you want to sculpt one that expresses the joy you have inside. You have to know the structure and scales of a blues song if you want to sing one that gets across your inner heartache. Your creative technique must be sufficient to support your complexity, emotion, vibrancy, and nuance.

If the scientist's aim is to create an internal understanding of the external world, the artist's aim is to create an external manifestation of her own interior world. When viewed this way, creativity and artistic endeavors are chiefly a journey of self-discovery, examining and discovering your feelings, desires, wishes, understandings, and messages, and *secondarily* an effort to express what you find. After all, if you aim to put your *self* into something—you'll need to know exactly who and what your *self* is.

You must also understand the traditions that create the context for your creation. A break with tradition is only meaningful if the artist and the audience are acutely aware of the tradition being broken. To think outside the box you have to know where the box is. Otherwise it's just ignorance!

For it to make the statement he intended, Duchamp had to put his famous *Fountain* in a *museum*. It would have had much less impact had he put it in, say, a wilderness area. Similarly, it would have had much less impact if he was a plumber with no ties to the art world and no artistic technique at all—even though no "technique" was directly used to create the object.

Creativity occurs at the edges, the boundaries, the borders.[8] It is what *pushes* the edges, boundaries, and borders. But you cannot push these if you're not already in dialogue with them. If you don't know how to follow them when it suits you. You can lead from ahead of the pack, or even from a mountaintop while your followers remain in the valley; but you cannot lead from another planet, in an alien language, with no understanding of the conventions of Earth.

The biggest leverage while investing in your creativity, then, will not come from arduously learning already existing techniques, or from letting loose in some wild, untrained fiesta-binge, but rather, from spending time and money in ways that cross-pollinate already existing ideas with fresh perspectives from differing fields, putting old ideas in new contexts, as Duchamp did. And from learning how to express more of your *self* in every small thing you do.

THE FOUR CONDITIONS OF CREATIVITY

Performers, athletes, writers, computer programmers, and professionals of all stripes attribute their most creative acts to being in "the zone." While they're in the zone, parts of themselves seem to disappear, and creativity moves through them, as if from a universal source, out into our world.

While the results of creativity are by definition unpredictable (otherwise they wouldn't be new or creative!), creativity itself arises from specific conditions—which are themselves predictable. That means that even if you don't think of yourself as a creative person, when those conditions are present, you will be able to tap into creative genius.

"The zone" is a by-product of these four conditions:

1. Spaciousness

Give yourself mental time and space. Allow time for the habitual thought patterns to dissipate. A friend of Bryan's, a highly creative and well-compensated executive at a cutting-edge LED company, does all his creative thinking on airplanes, because there he has the *mental spaciousness* that he can't do anything else with. Commute time on the train or in the car, shower time, and even just taking walks after a meal is great for this. Designate an area of your work space for creativity and keep it absolutely clear of debris. Do whatever it takes to give your mind the experience of spaciousness.

For this practice to be valuable, it is—ironically—necessary to separate the creative practice itself from any *practical* value or utilitarian outcome. This gives you the freedom to practice unbridled creativity. There are plenty of areas of life where we allow ourselves to have utility without creativity. We want you to have one area focused on creativity without utility. That will allow these areas to be balanced, so that when you go to use them together, you can.

As part of carving out a zone where you can practice creativity without any concern for practical utility, we recommend investing in becoming proficient in one artistic medium, simply for its own sake. Get good enough that your relation to the technique is not the dominant thing in your mind; you are instead able to get in the zone with that medium, the space of creating without thinking. Over many years of practice and self-investment, Bryan has mastered the arts of jazz piano improvisation and electronic music production, to the point where he can engage in these in a state of pure flow, without concern for technical abilities. Over the same period, Michael has learned to enter deep states of flow and creativity through writing, and also through Cuban salsa dance. Whether it's music, dance, writing, painting, or any other medium, we recommend mastering the technique of at least one discipline enough so that most of your thought is about *what* you want to express, rather than how to express it via technique.

This is a potent experience of creativity that will inform almost every other area of your life once you get there. If you have that practice, then when you're called to be creative in another nontraditional creative context, such as at work, you'll have little difficulty with that translation.

Can dance classes or singing lessons be a great investment? Yes. If you stick with it long enough to get seriously engaged with the creative process by doing so (rather than simply staying at the level of rote moves or songs), and if you allow that creativity to seep into the rest of your work, we believe these can be better investments than the stock market, by a long shot.

2. Constraints

The reason most sequels are not as good as the originals isn't that the filmmakers run out of ideas. It's because they usually have significantly more time, money, and latitude from the studio for the second movie. The first one was a huge success, so budgets and egos expand. Then, as the constraints decrease, the quality of creativity decreases as well. The beauty of human creativity is born of the constraints of being human. From arbitrary deadlines to iambic pentameter, find constraints that inspire your creative mind.

If you want to make any project more creative, start arbitrarily adding constraints. Want to get creative at building slide presentations? Try this rule: No more than three words per slide. Want them to be even more creative? Add a new rule: Only use verbs and adjectives. Do they still feel bland? Try summarizing each slide into a single word, and find an image (a quick Internet images search using your word will do the trick) instead of printing the word. Want to go even further? Try using pictures that have the exact *opposite* meaning that you wish to convey (like a picture of a championship trophy when you are communicating that you lost a large account, or a picture of a Formula One car to communicate that you think the QA team should slow down and do more careful work). By adding just a few constraints, you've saved coworkers who might otherwise have been victims of death-by-bullet-point.

3. Models of Inspiration

Inspiration basically comes in two forms. The first is "I want to be like you." Writers emulate writers. Musicians emulate musicians. Businesses emulate businesses. Choose someone who inspires you and study how he or she does everything. Neither compete against nor idolize your inspiration. Just observe. This is best for learning new ways to translate your ideas into form through technique. This kind of inspiration can teach you an "alphabet" by emulating the work of others that you can later use to form new words, phrases, and sentences.

The second form of inspiration is "I want to express what it's like to know you," a form of contextual importing. Ravel's "Une Barque sur l'Océan" is a musical expression of what it's like to be at sea. The huge iconic fins and bulbous chrome bumpers on American cars in the late 1950s were automotive expressions of the B-52 bomber. Crane-style, monkey style, and tiger-style are among the forms of kung fu inspired by the movements and temperaments of those animals.

Write like Monet. Work like a gladiator. Dance like a factory. Love like Bobby Fischer. Use contextual importing to transform old ideas into fresh, new ones. Be explicit about your inspiration and hold him/her/it in your mind as you create.

4. Loving Your Ideas into Existence

Each idea fragment that spills from your mind must be met by a resounding "YES!" The more you love the seedlings that sprout in your mind, the more fertile the mind itself becomes. Your objective is to open the channel between you and that unknown, unconscious source within you from which creativity springs, not to evaluate how the fruit will taste from the tree that might grow from the seed you see. Each "YES" loves the channel more open. Each "NO" closes it. Once each idea begins to develop and mature, step back and evaluate it. Until that point, your job is not to come up with good ideas, but to love every idea that you come up with.

The hardest part of loving your own ideas, for anyone taking their own creativity seriously, is the disheartening effect of comparing your creations with the way you imagined they could be before you made them. For all but the most accomplished creative technicians, there is a pretty big gap between how the painting (or song, or poem, or book chapter, or dance, etc.) looked in their head before they started painting and how it looks on the canvas once the paint is dry. It takes emotional resilience not to quit in that moment. To not say "NO" to your own idea.

It may help to remember that you are the only one who can see the way you wished it had turned out, and everyone else who might see it will have no such reference with which to judge your work. When expressing your creativity and feeling the gap, strive to do this: feel the impulse to quit, keep going anyway, and promise to invest in a new level of technical ability that will help close the gap in the future. As electronic music producer Phutureprimitive (Bryan's favorite musical artist and biggest musical influence) says, "Just keep working on your craft until what comes out of the speakers sounds just like what was in your head in the first place."

THE BEST WAY TO BOOST YOUR CREATIVITY: **COMFORT WITH UNCERTAINTY AND "LOOKING WEIRD"**

For something to be creative, it must be new. If it is not new in some significant way (even as it draws on older influences, as all creativity does), then it is not creative, but rather, copying.

Yet, when producing new ideas or creations, you are taking a risk. Something could be new but worthless. Coming to work with bird poop on your shoulder is new, but worthless. Yet, even if your new creation does not involve the digestive tract of birds, there is always the risk that it will be met with a similar reaction as bird poop on your shoulder.

Which is precisely why most people avoid creativity. Most people are raised in families that encourage conformity to family values and norms. (This is not a criticism of parenting—it would be difficult to raise children *without* encouraging this to some degree.) Our training in conformity continues on the playground, where some are viciously attacked for any deviation from the clique's social norms. And in the classroom, where teachers, for reasons of curriculum compliance as well as classroom management, discourage any thinking, behavior, or lifestyle choices that swerve outside of preordained thought patterns.

As Michael wrote about in *The Education of Millionaires*, by the time we exit college, we've had nearly every last drop of the boundless, unruly creativity of our childhoods wrung out of us, and if we want any back in our adulthood, we must reclaim it.

One of the most powerful ways to do that is to invite unpredictability into your life. Most of our lives, we have clung to choices that provide more certainty in education, travel, mates, careers. None of this is wrong in itself. But it is a death knell for creativity. There is a reason that artists for centuries have been drawn to tempestuous relationships, exotic and potentially

dangerous foreign lands, far-out philosophical and spiritual belief systems, altered states of consciousness, and living in edgy,
rough neighborhoods. Very few things are more important to creativity than receiving unexpected, unusual, surprising stimuli
that challenge your normal thought patterns.

Have you ever been on a vacation where you had a "tourist
checklist"? You go to a foreign land, where you are supposed to
be having foreign experiences, and before you even arrive,
you've got a vision of what your experience is supposed to look
like. That is exactly the opposite of the type of travel—and the
type of experience in general—we recommend for increasing
your comfort with uncertainty.

Attempting to remain in control of everything is the enemy
of creativity. All of the seriously creative people we know talk
about creativity as something that "flows through them." The
main task of the creative is to "open the channel" so that creative
ideas coming from who-knows-where (the subconscious? the
muse? a divine spark?) may flow in full force. It is the process
of humbly allowing the unknown to bubble up in your consciousness.

That which is creative cannot be known in advance. When
you find yourself on the edges of uncertainty, move toward the
unknown and say "Yes!" Your mind will likely serve up a hundred reasons to say no. "You might look weird," "Other people
are better than you," "You might offend someone," or "What if
they hate it?" If you listen, then you keep the unknown, and
creativity with it, at a safe distance. Don't listen.

This, obviously, requires comfort with the unknown. There
is nothing that will hinder your creativity faster than demanding to know what the products of your creativity will be before
you create them. The creative act is like answering "Yes!" first,
and then hearing the question afterward. Imagine saying "Yes!"
to every offer or suggestion made to you, regardless of its source,

even before you know what it is, for a day, a week, or even a lifetime. As you contemplate *actually doing* something like that, a nervous energy wells up from your gut and percolates up toward your chest. That energy is actually *creative* energy, "mislabeled" as fear about the future in your body.

If you say "No," the energy dissipates and you return to homeostasis in your body chemistry. If you say "Yes," the energy can peak. It's as if it starts to flow out of you and manifest in the world (in the form of your new experience or creation). Once it has manifested, then the energy is dissipated, and your body again returns to homeostasis. If your goal in life is to have neutral body chemistry, then say "No" a lot more often. If your goal is to invest in your creativity, then strive to make your default answer "Yes!" and learn to get comfortable with the feelings of energy in your body that go with that answer.

Of course, sometimes the prudent answer is no, and there are times when planning ahead and reducing risk are more beneficial than increasing creativity. (We'd much prefer our surgeon to be more bound by training and tradition than by sudden inspiration to try something new. We prefer our car mechanic to think inside the box as well.) But chances are, across many areas of life we've erred way too far on the safe side.

The next time you take a trip, go somewhere that interests you, but put the itinerary and the guides away. Wander and subject yourself to random, unpredictable experiences and people.

Devote some of your time to socializing with people way outside of your comfort zone. If you're a buttoned-up manager, find a way to socialize with the freaky-artistic-bohemian crowd. If you're an artistic bohemian, go socialize with the people at the libertarian meetup. Expose yourself to radically different ways of seeing and thinking about the world. If you're single and dating, consider dating people *way outside* your cultural box. Even if you don't end up in a relationship with them, you'll immerse yourself in new ideas, and you'll end up with a wider perspective and more creative inspiration.

Read books and Web sites by people you disagree with. In fact, read books that infuriate you. Read Web forums populated by people of entirely different cultures and subcultures, debating issues you know nothing about. Say "YES!" to life's variety and creativity will say "YES!" to you.

CREATIVE SUPER SKILL: Improvisation

Improvisation is the discipline of thinking on your feet, under pressure. You can think of it as applied uncertainty. To do it, you must be *very* comfortable with the unknown, as you literally might not know what will come out of your mouth two seconds in advance! It is an incredibly useful skill for anyone who must lead teams, present, pitch, or sell. It can teach you to say "YES" and to acclimate to elevated levels of creative energy in your body. Even if you get no other benefits, improvisation qualifies as a Super Skill—enhancing the value of all your other skills—simply by teaching you how to stay present, focused, and generative under pressure.

When you can't handle the nervous energy or other sensations in your body, you lose access to (some of) your higher cognitive functions, as in a fight/flight response, and end up unconsciously taking the shortest path to returning to neutral body chemistry. You might break the tension with a nervous laugh, or try to run away. The higher the levels of body sensation you can allow yourself while maintaining relaxed access to your creative and reasoning faculties, the higher-value situations you can be trusted to handle. Bryan's wife Jennifer, who also trains entrepreneurs to show up more powerfully in high-intensity situations, calls it "holding sensation."

Once you start investing in your ability to hold sensation calmly, you can seek out high-value experiences that most people avoid because they are afraid. Holding sensation is the key to poise, grace, confidence, and even increasing your personal power and sexual attraction. Improvisation is an excellent entry point for that pursuit.

While there are many ways to learn improvisation—music, dance, stand-up—probably the most accessible and relevant for everyone is learning improvisational acting. Look up "improv classes" online in your local area and you'll probably find many options catering to all tastes and experience levels. A few months and a few hundred dollars invested in this way will likely give you an entirely different relationship to nervousness and the experience of not knowing what to say next, and a safe environment to practice holding sensation.

CREATIVE SUPER SKILL: **Writing**

A common bit of faux-wisdom holds that, given decreasing attention spans and the fusion-implanting of multimedia devices in everyone's palms, reading and writing are dead. You should all learn how to make YouTube videos, says this piece of modern wisdom—and make them short at that (with lots of effects and cartoons to grab our attention!).

Yet, to paraphrase one of history's master writers (and readers), Mark Twain, the reports of the death of writing and reading were greatly exaggerated. The Internet is still primarily a *written* medium. No matter how many videos populate the Web, written words still predominate, and we don't see that changing anytime soon.

While video cover letters are gaining popularity, can you imagine a job interview process for a significant management position that involves *zero* examples of the candidates' writing? Can you imagine someone being an effective leader of an organization while being a totally ineffective writer?

On the contrary, knowing how to write compelling and persuasive e-mails, letters, memos, proposals, and pitches is one of the most effective skills you could develop for your career and business. Virtually every transaction gets mediated through some kind of text, whether it is e-mail, Web copy, or a video script. Writing well in these media sets you apart from your competitors. It doesn't matter how good your ideas are if you can't communicate them. For the reader, the unclear writer is indistinguishable from the unclear thinker.

Think of all the people who influence your career, and who must process volumes of prose: potential employers who wade through your cover letters and résumés, potential investors who wade through your business proposals, potential team members who decide whether to support your project at work, potential customers who wade through your Web copy or promotional e-mails.

The quantity of bad business prose that gets written each year is exceeded only by the quantity of smoke blown by politicians. Vague. Flaccid. Shapeless. Rambling. Without point or purpose.

"Our bandwidth center is focused on new ways to quantify the consumer space through out of the box deployments of corporate social responsibility." This was not, in fact, a press release. Rather, it was a randomly generated sentence on *The Wall Street Journal*'s "Business Buzzwords Generator." That you've probably read countless pronouncements in the business media that sound just like this, however, highlights the problem.[9]

When you're in a position of reading (and passing judgment on) high volumes of prose, and—by some miracle—a piece of crisp, alive, human prose manages to sparkle through the truckloads of muck, all you can do is throw your hands up and rejoice. And grant the writer her request.

You might think that writing is basically a "college-level" skill, and that you learned everything you need to know to write well in college. Unfortunately (for all but the most committed students of the Creative Super Skill of writing), despite the amount of writing you do in college, you're about as likely to leave having learned to write clear, compelling prose as you're likely to leave a college kegger without stinking of beer.

An article in *The Wall Street Journal* entitled "M.B.A. Recruiters' No. 1 Pet Peeve: Poor Writing and Speaking Skills" puts the problem bluntly: "For Chris Aisenbrey, director of global university relations at Whirlpool Corp., it's a daunting challenge these days to hire literate M.B.A. students who can write a coherent letter or memo. Too often, what he gets from job applicants are collections of rambling thoughts littered with misspellings and grammatical gaffes. . . . Of all the complaints recruiters register about M.B.A. students in *The Wall Street Journal*/Harris Interactive survey, inferior communication skills top the list."[10]

This article implies that poor communication skills fresh out of school result from simple laziness or stupidity. But Dr. Richard Lanham, professor emeritus of English at UCLA, believes the problem is not lack of learning. Rather, he believes, when we are undergraduates, we *learn all too well:* we learn to ape the bureaucratic, academic, clear-as-swamp-water prose of our professors. He writes in his book *Revising Prose:* "Much bad writing today comes not from the conventional sources of verbal dereliction—sloth, original sin, or native absence of mind—but from stylistic imitation. It is learned, an act of stylistic piety, which imitates a single style, the bureaucratic style I have called *The Official Style. . . .* Nobody feels comfortable writing simply 'Boy meets Girl.' The system requires something like 'A romantic relationship is ongoing between Boy and Girl.' Or 'Boy and Girl are currently implementing an interactive romantic relationship.'"[11]

If you want to write well, usually you must teach yourself. Fortunately, there are many excellent books and courses that can help you. Here are two options:

1. *Writing with Power: Techniques for Mastering the Writing Process* by Peter Elbow

Elbow encourages you to separate the *writing* process from the *revising* process—as they require two entirely different mental faculties. He gives great guidance for enhancing each. Here's Michael's own analogy of the process he learned from Elbow in this book: Writing is like a wild party; revising is like cleaning up the party. Ideally, you don't mix the two. The best partying (and writing) happens when you let go of all constraint, let your mind and body and imagination and creativity run wild, don't pay heed to any pieties or proprieties, and don't hold anything back. The best cleaning up of the party (and the best editing) occurs *after*, not during—ideally after the intoxication (natural or otherwise) has passed through your system and you've had a cold shower and a strong cup of coffee. You can then roll up your sleeves, get the rubber gloves and disinfectant, and clean up last night's beautiful mess.

2. *Revising Prose* by Richard Lanham

Learn to cut out what Lanham calls the "Lard Factor" present in most specimens of university-taught writing. The Lard Factor is the ~~percentage of~~ excess verbiage you should ~~be able to~~ cut from your ~~otherwise flaccid~~ prose through ~~extremely well-intentioned, high quality,~~ good revision.

Writing is a valuable Super Skill in its own right, honing your ability to construct complete thoughts and represent your ideas and experiences vividly, but it also has a unique mutant ability to change (not just enhance the value of) other Super Skills.

Writing combined with other Super Skills spawns specialized disciplines, each with its own amplification effect on your earning potential.

Writing + Marketing Crank (revealed in the next chapter) = Content Marketing, the skill of using blog posts and other content to generate new customer leads for any business at near-zero acquisition costs. More than a trillion dollars is spent each year on customer acquisition by American businesses, to give you some idea of the potential value of this particular "mutant" skill.

Writing + Public Speaking = Speech Writing, which, once mastered, becomes an all-access pass to networking with leaders of all stripes.

Writing + Visioning + Teaching = Nonfiction Authorship, which leads to a step-function leap in credibility and reach.

Writing + Selling = Copywriting, the highest dollar-per-word earning potential in the universe of professional communication (with the possible exception of Johnny Depp's performance in the movie *Edward Scissorhands,* for which he earned a multimillion-dollar payday while uttering just 169 words).

CREATIVE SUPER SKILL: Copywriting

Copywriting is any writing designed to produce a specific action, such as buying something, clicking on something, or joining a list. It is singular in purpose—to compel the reader to act—and more quantitative than qualitative as a discipline. If the goal of writing is to faithfully represent your interior thoughts and feelings for the reader, copywriting is like "inside out" writing, requiring you to faithfully represent the interior thoughts and feelings of the *reader.* And based on the personal experience of these authors, learning how to be a copywriter can *feel* like you're turning your brain inside out! Like writing with your nondominant hand or learning the proper pronunciation of words in a foreign language, the early days of investing in copywriting can be slow, awkward, and frustrating.

However, the reward for sticking with it and making it past the hump (of perhaps one hundred to five hundred hours of practice) is like the moment when Neo first "sees" the Matrix in the movie of the same name. Suddenly the inner workings of traffic patterns on the Internet, customer behavior patterns, patterns of favoritism and influence at the office, and even patterns of romantic mate selection become "visible," predictable, and inalienable by your hand. In the well-chosen words of Keanu Reeves as Neo, "Whoa."

There was a time when discussing copywriting would have made more sense in the chapter on Technical Super Skills. There were a few time-tested formulas of persuasion that, if applied in almost any circumstance, produced results. However, the online ecosystem has changed. After ten years of hundreds of thousands of people taking aggressively marketed courses on copywriting, the Net is flooded with mediocre, repetitive, formulaic marketing copy, most of which is producing poorer and poorer results.

Now, to be persuasive, your copy must be *original* and have *personality*. It must communicate the values of the brand as well as motivate action (more on this in chapter 5's rendering of "Direct Marketing"). The downside is that it takes lots of practice to learn how to produce original, lively, persuasive copy. The upside is that if you invest the time and money to learn how to do so, you will be rewarded with ample opportunity to boost your earning potential, as there is so much bad, unoriginal copy flooding the Web. (If you are interested in learning how to write copy, Michael's last book, *The Education of Millionaires*, provides an extensive guide, in chapter 4, on how to give yourself a low-cost education in copywriting.)

CREATIVE SUPER SKILL: **Reading**

If you want to cook a great-tasting meal, there's no substitute for good ingredients. If you want to be creative in the realm of ideas, there is simply no substitute for reading. Through reading, you have access to all the highest-quality human thought in recorded history, for your immediate consumption as the raw material—as the ingredients—of your creative thinking.

No creative idea emerges from the thinker's mind out of whole cloth. Encountering and grappling with the ideas of others is required to come up with your own ideas. And, unless you are fortunate enough to have constant access to the minds of geniuses as you sit at home, there is no easier, more accessible, and less expensive way to access those minds than reading books. The ideas you will gain from reading are the building blocks you will use to form your own original, creative ideas in the workplace, and beyond.

Billionaire Charlie Munger, Warren Buffett's right-hand man as vice-chairman of Berkshire Hathaway, who—along with the Oracle of Omaha himself—is considered one of the greatest investors of all time, writes: "In my whole life, I have known no wise people who didn't read all the time—none, zero. You'd be amazed at how much Warren reads—at how much I read. My children laugh at me. They think I'm a book with a couple of legs sticking out."[12]

Successful people invest time reading biographies of great men and women throughout history (legendary leaders, thinkers, scientists, entrepreneurs, philosophers, writers, artists, athletes, musicians) for inspiration. They read about psychology, self-help, and personal development so they can better grasp their own inner worlds and the inner demons that may keep them back from success—and also so they can better understand the minds of their competition. They read books on spirituality so they may strengthen the roots of their deepest values and find guidance in their lives. They read philosophy so they may sharpen their minds. They read popular science and current affairs so they are on top of the latest discoveries and developments. They read books on marketing, sales, persuasion, and leadership so they may master the disciplines essential for bringing their visions to the world.

If you want more creativity in your life, and/or if you want to improve a certain area of your life, whether it's finances, health, relationships, or career, we know of no surer (or more cost-effective or simple) investment than immersing yourself in a wide range of books on the topic. Don't stop at reading a single book with a single point of view. Read books that attack each other. Read totally opposing perspectives.

From this cacophony of opinions, argument, research, and conflicting viewpoints in any given field, a path that is right for you will emerge, we promise. It may not reveal itself immediately, but keep reading, and it will. All those background ideas and opinions and arguments ricocheting in your mind from your wide-ranging reading will serve as the building blocks to your own unique solutions, creations, and brilliance.

"But I Don't Have Time to Read!": How to "Read" Four to Eight Books per Month with No Extra Time

This passionate call-to-reading may sound great in theory. But how can it work in practice, given how much time reading takes and how little free time you have?

Your e-mail is coming in like heavy artillery. Your cell phone has morphed into a remote-control vibrator permanently buzzing in your pocket or purse. Your business, family, and social schedule make your electronic calendar jam more than Charlie Parker. In the midst of all this chaos, how on Earth would you ever get a chance to read?

Well, here's a solution. Most of us manage to find hours a day for listening to the same worries, dramas, or regrets play over and over again on the radio station in our minds: While commuting in traffic. While at the gym. While shopping for groceries. While chopping vegetables.

You may not have much time to sit down and read anymore. But all you have to do is switch off the twenty-four-hour worry channel in your head, pull out your iPod, smartphone, or other digital player, and switch on the audiobooks. An hour on the train, ten minutes waiting at the post office, fifteen minutes washing dishes, forty-five minutes at the gym, twelve minutes while folding the laundry, thirty minutes while you are drifting off to sleep: all these moments contain what we call "underutilized aural capacity." These moments of free aural (but not visual) attention are the classic definition of an underutilized resource, the basis of good business investing: a resource that can be put to much better use.

Become an expert at stealing these moments for audiobooks, and it can add up to hours a day you never knew you had for learning. Most nonfiction books weigh in at seven to nine hours in audiobook form. If you can steal just an hour a day for listening (easy to do if you commute and/or do errands, cooking, exercise, etc.), that adds up to about a book a week, or fifty-two books a year. If you can find two or three hours a day while you go about your life, that adds up to around two books a week, or more than a hundred per year.

Charles Eliot, president of Harvard University from 1869 to 1909, said that "a five-foot shelf would hold books enough to give in the course of years a good substitute for a liberal education in youth to anyone who would read them with devotion, even if he could spare but fifteen minutes a day for reading."[13] Little did he expect that that same library, available in audio, could now fit on a five-gigabyte iPhone, five inches long, and that the average person would have not minutes, but underutilized *hours* every day to listen.

Here are some masterful nonfiction books available in audiobook format to get you started, and to get creative ideas in various areas of your career rolling. Each of these books contains paradigm-shifting ideas that had a profound, immediate, and permanent effect on us.

Business/Sales/Marketing
- *SPIN Selling* by Neil Rackham—In our opinion, the best single book on sales.
- *Scientific Advertising* by Claude Hopkins—The classic bible of direct response marketing.
- *Building a Small Business That Warren Buffett Would Love* by Adam Brownlee—A wonderful book that applies the investment criteria of legendary investor Warren Buffett to entrepreneurship.
- *The Five Dysfunctions of a Team* by Patrick Lencioni—The clearest book about how to create a high-functioning team; it will show you exactly what's wrong with a team and what to do about it.
- *Good to Great* by Jim Collins—The best book on separating myth from fact regarding what actually makes great business leadership.

Relationships and Networking (Business and Personal)
- *Never Eat Alone* by Keith Ferrazzi (with Tahl Raz), and *Who's Got Your Back* by Keith Ferrazzi (with Max

Alexander)—The two best books on networking and relationship building as essential parts of one's career.

- *Mating in Captivity: Unlocking Erotic Intelligence* by Esther Perel—The best book on the problems facing modern couples, and how to fix them.

Miscellaneous

- *Fooled by Randomness: The Hidden Role of Chance in Life and in the Markets* and *The Black Swan: The Impact of the Highly Improbable* by Nassim Nicholas Taleb—These books will get you to see life, risk, financial markets, investing, and just about everything in a new light.
- *The Power of Habit: Why We Do What We Do in Life and Business* by Charles Duhigg—This book shows you how most everything in your life is based on habit, and how to change habits for the better.
- *The Fourth Turning: An American Prophecy* by William Strauss and Neil Howe—The best book diagnosing the age/generation wars in the distribution of opportunity and wealth, to which our SAFE plan is an alternative.
- *The UltraMind Solution: The Simple Way to Defeat Depression, Overcome Anxiety, and Sharpen Your Mind* by Mark Hyman, MD—The best book on diet and nutrition as they relate to mental performance, focus, energy, and mood.

CREATIVE SUPER SKILL: Storytelling

Imagine that you had a supernatural power to *install* meaning in other people's minds. Imagine that you could, through some flick of the wrist, make any object or event contain any significance, meaning, or interpretation you wanted. You could cause people to fall in love, to make huge investments, to go to war, to make peace, to work late or go home early. Sounds like the kind of ability a storyteller might give a comic book villain (too powerful an ability to give to the hero). You could easily rob a bank by making the meaning of "life threatening," you could get your dream spouse to propose to you by making the meaning of "soul mate," you could get any promotion you want by making the meaning "most valuable employee," and end up ruling the world! (Insert evil laugh here.)

But! Every superpower has a limitation (for the purposes of making the comic book story interesting). In this case, we'll make the limitation that you can only install meanings in other people that are authentic for you—meanings that you also believe. If you use your power to mislead people, installing meanings that you know to be false or less desirable, your power *overheats* and eventually blows up in your face like a grenade.

Still, it's a pretty awesome superpower. Robbing the bank probably won't work, but you wouldn't want to, because you'd be able to make the meaning of happiness, love, and significance. If you fell in love, you could still get the proposal from the dream spouse, and if you believed you deserved it, you would still get the promotion. You'd never again have the experience that something was important to you, but not important to someone else.

This is, in fact, a good approximation of the power of good storytelling. It's at the very heart of sales, marketing, advice, coaching, product design, leadership, politics (office or otherwise), media, and influence, not to mention romance, entertainment, and art, making it an essential Super Skill. If you add storytelling to almost any piece of communication, it has more impact. So investing in becoming a good storyteller isn't just for fun or entertainment, it is for creating more impact in any area of your life that involves communication.

The best way to become a master storyteller (other than the obvious investments of books, workshops, and online courses) is to pay attention to great storytellers. When a friend or colleague is telling a great story, pay attention to what they omit. Pay attention to the sequence of obscuring and revealing facts of the story. How do they begin? How do they end? When do they pause? When do they rush? Then try to retell the same story to a different group and see if you get a similar reaction. Doing this repeatedly will help you see the patterns that are common to all good stories, allowing you to start to craft your own meaning-making machines.

Joseph Campbell, author and mythologist, devoted his life to studying those story patterns until 1949, when he made possibly the most significant contribution to the field of storytelling since the invention of the campfire. In his book *The Hero with a Thousand Faces*, Campbell outlines what he calls the *monomyth*, popularly known as the *hero's journey*, which draws structural parallels between all major hero myths (or stories), including the stories of Jesus, Buddha, and Krishna, characterizing them as *basically the same myth*, but with different character names, costumes, and set dressing. In fact, almost all popular myths, plays, novels, and movies conform to the stages (think of them as major plot points) in the hero's journey described by Campbell.

A shortcut to becoming a great storyteller could be to do what George Lucas famously did when conceiving of *Star Wars*. Sit down with the *monomyth* as a wire frame for your story and then fill in the details for color. (There is a wonderful book that teaches how to do this, called *The Writer's Journey* by Christopher Vogler.) Campbell must have been complimented, because his book was reprinted sporting a picture of Luke Skywalker (actor Mark Hamill) on the cover.[14]

CREATIVE SUPER SKILL: **Design**

Design is storytelling without words.

A well-designed Web site effortlessly guides your attention where and when it is needed. Somehow it gives you all the information you want, with no distractions, and leads you to take the actions that the owner of the site wants from you.

A well-designed car not only changes how you feel about the car when you drive it but it can change how you feel about *yourself* when you drive it. Frugal, sporty, luxurious, eco-friendly. These attributes are more commonly communicated through the car's design than through its actual mechanical attributes.

A well-designed environment inspires the kind of interactions and conversations that the designer most wished for the space, at the pace, frequency, and intensity the designer felt would be optimal.

The difference between a well-designed casino layout and a poor design is the difference between record-breaking profits (in the case of the Wynn Las Vegas) and bankruptcy (in the case of the Aladdin, which diverted arriving guests around the moneymaking gaming floor).

Engineering is governed entirely by function. Art is governed entirely by form, or aesthetics. Design is the marriage between function and form. Good design integrates them into one inseparable experience. Like storytelling, design tells us how to feel, what meaning to make, and what is expected of us. If the function of a Web site, for example, is to sell a product, but the design contains too many competing visual elements, each a part of a different storyline about what a visitor is supposed to do next and what the visitor is supposed to think and feel about the product, the visitor is left with two options. Either give up and leave or become a detective, carefully scanning the page like a proofreader hunting for the next action he wants to take (a tiny percentage of visitors take this second option).

There's a shared concept that designers tend to strive for, something we call "Design Utopia." The quality of a design is basically a measurement of how close the designers were able to get to the unattainable Design Utopia within the given resource and technological constraints. In Design Utopia, the following are executed flawlessly:

1. CONVERTING IMPULSES TO MET NEEDS.

The object wraps itself around the user (metaphorically, perhaps) and senses the user's desires, needs, and impulses. If the user wants to start using the product, and her impulse is to feel in the back for a power button, the Utopian product senses the *impulse* to feel toward the back—perhaps before her hand actually touches the object—and turns the device on. In Design Utopia, everything works the way you think it might, and the designers thought it all up in advance.

2. REMOVING ANYTHING UNESSENTIAL.

There is absolutely nothing extra in Design Utopia. No extraneous buttons, lines, words, pieces, steps, or shapes. One minimalist solution solves many problems. You can usually improve a design by taking something out; rarely by adding something new. *Graphic Design for Nondesigners* by Tony Seddon is a great reference text to help you understand just how much extra stuff you habitually include in your documents, presentations, Web pages, and images.

3. EVOKING THE INTENDED MEANING,

including feelings and conclusions. Meaning is created wordlessly by the relationship between the object's design and its cultural context. It doesn't belong to the design itself. A great design for a sport coat in

1974 would probably not seem so great today. A perfectly designed ceiling fan in your house would be a design disaster on a submarine. In Design Utopia, the object evokes the intended meaning in its proper context, which is reinforced by trends that feel current and even new.

To begin your investment in the Creative Super Skill of design, look around at the products in your home. How close do they get to Design Utopia? Do they respond well to your impulses (like a refrigerator—just grab the handle to open, put something on a shelf to make it cold)? Has everything unessential been removed (like a chessboard or a frying pan)? Do you feel what you imagine the creators of the object would hope for you to feel when using it? Are you confident in the object, its brand, and the results or outcomes it promises? Start to focus on the Web sites, brochures, and items around the house that feel unnecessarily far from Design Utopia. If you start to let your imagination fix products that miss the mark, you'll start to understand the elements and impact of design.

Today the skill of design is integrated into every aspect of products and the marketing assets that promote them, from conception to construction to consumption. We predict that the biggest opportunities to deliver value (and increase your earning potential) will be further integrating Design Utopian thinking directly into every business process, rather than marketing yourself as having "design skills" on the side.

No matter what you're up to in your career, it is highly likely that you will need to produce persuasive content, whether it is a pitch, a presentation, a Web site, or a prototype of a physical product. Persuasive content serves the function of compelling people to take a singular, very high-value action: invest, buy, decide, acquire, join, approve, or recommend. The design can tell the story of *why* your listeners and readers should take that action. It can *show* rather than *tell* important parts of your story that might not work as well if you spoke them directly, such as "I'm good at my job," "We make a lot of money at this company," "Important people trust us," or "You shouldn't worry about our past failures, because tomorrow is a new day!"

Design is becoming a more influential factor in buying decisions for consumers and companies alike. Even industries that seemed immune from (and devoid of) design as a decisive factor, such as enterprise software (where green screen applications went to die, and user experience [UX] tracks fifteen years or more behind consumer software), are now competing on design, thanks to forward-looking companies like Salesforce.com and Agilecockpit.com. This expansion of potential design projects with higher and higher expectations is leaving a broadening talent shortage of good designers. Turn this talent gap into economic opportunity for you by investing seriously in your design ability as a complement to your other Market and Super Skills.

EXTRA-CREDIT CREATIVITY INVESTMENT: The Burn

Finally, there is a reason large parts of the business elite of the world's most innovative entrepreneurial ecosystem—Silicon Valley—go to Burning Man each year, the famous weeklong community and arts festival in the Nevada desert. (Both of us have been yards away from Sergey Brin, cofounder of Google, doing a downward-facing-dog yoga pose, his face inches away from the dusty desert ground, at Burning Man.) We believe that everyone who is seriously interested in increasing their range of creativity should attend Burning Man at least once in their life. It is, in our opinion, the greatest concentration of creative energy ever put together in one place, and few people leave "The

Burn" without having their sense of what is possible for them massively expanded.

Over the course of a few days, tens of thousands of people seem to create any crazy idea they can possibly dream up (from twenty-foot flaming iron orchid statues, to a functional replica of the Thunderdome from the Mad Max movies, to a giant glowing yellow duck on wheels made from an old transit bus). With such a high concentration of creative people loving their ideas into existence, the feeling of acceptance permeates the festival. Self-acceptance, acceptance of others, and acceptance of uncertainty. In short, it's a high-concentration environment of "Yes!"

Could spending several thousand dollars to attend a party in the desert (including ticket, travel, and supplies) be a good investment? For a person who's never been, who wants to enhance earning potential by bringing more creativity and more of *themselves* to their work, who might professionally benefit from meeting innovative entrepreneurs on the leading edge of popular culture, or who wants to increase their ability to hold sensation, it's hard to imagine a better way to invest. In short, "Yes."

CHAPTER 5

INVEST IN TECHNICAL SUPER SKILLS

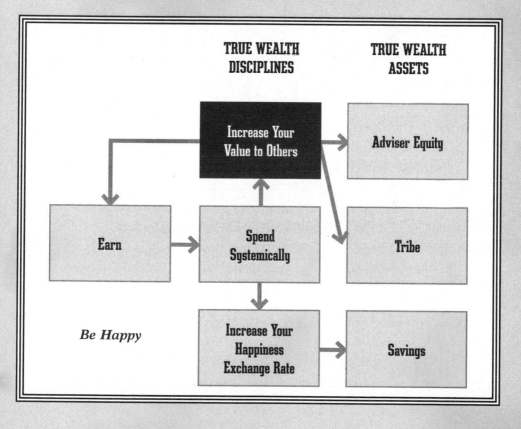

■ MENTAL MODELS ■

■ FINANCIAL MODELS ■

■ SYSTEMS THINKING ■

■ BUILDING A MARKETING CRANK ■

"**C**an you build twenty-eight cell sites in six months?"

This might seem like an ordinary question for a cell phone company to ask a construction contractor in a preliminary meeting about a potential project. But it was far from ordinary. First of all, it was San Diego, 1998, and there were only two cell phone carriers at the time in the area. It was understood that unless these twenty-eight new sites (think of them as sophisticated radio towers that make up the cellular network) could be built by this deadline around the city, the company was going to lose *all* of its 200,000-plus subscribers to its one competitor.

Second, it was Lee Franklin's (Bryan's father) first day on the job as president of J. Whalen Associates, the construction contractor being asked the question. Lee had been a successful entrepreneur and executive in the telecommunications industry, but until that day had never led a construction project larger than remodeling his own kitchen. He had also never even *seen* a cell site. "The closest I had gotten to the cell phone business at that time was using a cell phone to make calls."

Dan Whalen, founder of J. Whalen Associates and the man who hired Lee to be president, was the first to break the silence. "How long does it normally take to build *one* cell site?"

"Eighteen months," reported a nervous technical adviser in the room.

"So," the cell phone company executive replied. "We need twenty-eight new cell sites in six months. Can you do it?"

What happened next shocked Lee and set in motion one of the most important learning experiences of his life.

Dan simply said, "Yes."

Lee saw everyone's shoulders in the room drop two inches

in one collective sigh of relief. Everyone's shoulders, that is, but his own.

"How are you going to do it?" asked the client, expecting an answer akin to pulling a rabbit out of a hat right there in the executive suite. Having no idea what Dan was about to say, Lee was as interested as the clients to learn what magic trick Dan had in mind to pull off this modern miracle:

"I don't know. But Lee is going to figure it out."

Lee didn't have the technical *Market* Skills to figure out how to do what people who were in the industry for decades thought was impossible. Technical Market Skills are basically "know-how." Skills like knowing *how* the equipment in the cell towers worked, *how* to coordinate a big-budget construction project, or *how* to navigate the local politics involved in San Diego city planning. Each one of these skills can take years, if not decades, to master. Obviously, on this compressed time schedule, there was no time to learn any of the Technical Market Skills a person would need to be successful at the task at hand. Without the requisite "know-how," perhaps it was his Interpersonal Super Skills of leadership and salesmanship that had gotten Lee the opportunity to sit in that room, and that had persuaded Dan and the cell phone company to place their faith in Lee. After all, he had led successful companies and large divisions before. But Interpersonal Skills couldn't build twenty-eight cell sites in six months. To pull this off, there would need to be some radical innovation, and innovation takes *know-how.*

Most people let the limits of their technical knowledge limit their career path, their value to others, and their earning potential. People who don't *know how* finance works stay away from positions that would require them to learn financial skills— even though those positions may be more lucrative or fulfilling.

Entrepreneurs who don't *know how* marketing works on the Internet tend to build business that can't scale quickly and struggle to find new customers. People without a solid technical understanding in their field tend to gravitate to (often lower-compensated) service roles that support the main business, but are not directly involved in it. They tend to define themselves as "nontechnical" and then stay that way because they fail to invest in technical knowledge.

Knowing how things work has the effect of making obstacles seem smaller and opportunities seem greater. If your car breaks down in the middle of nowhere with a mess of tools and no help in sight, and you *know how* cars work, this is a minor setback. If you don't, it's a potentially life-threatening challenge. If you are starting a new business and you *know how* to use Internet marketing effectively, the challenge of getting new customers is a minor one. If you don't, it could easily lead to failure and bankruptcy. This kind of *know-how* is usually hard-won—the result of hundreds or even thousands of hours of self-investment. It's also tremendously valuable, acting as a multiplier on your value to others and, by extension, your earning potential.

If you ask Lee if he's a technical person, he says, "No, but I know how to work well with technical people, and they love working with me." This is because of his Technical Super Skills—which like all other Super Skills enhance the value of all your other skills. Technical Super Skills, if you invest in them, give you the ability to solve technical problems, even if you identify as a "nontechnical" person. Perhaps the most powerful of these skills is the know-how to know how, or the ability to build an effective *mental model*. This is the ability to develop just enough technical understanding to work intimately and effectively with technical people and create technical innovations.

This works; not because you've learned everything there is to know about the technical details in that field, and not because you're smarter than those who have tried before, but because you've built an effective mental model and used that model to understand how things work. If you know how to build mental models, you know how to learn how just about anything works, from organic chemistry to computer software to nanotechnology to financial business systems. The Technical Super Skill of building mental models is like a shortcut to the value multiplier of know-how that can be achieved in hours or days instead of years or decades.

THE MOST POWERFUL TECHNICAL SUPER SKILL:
BUILDING MENTAL MODELS

A mental model is very much like a model airplane or an architect's model. It is a simplified functional representation of something larger and more complex. That's useful because such a model is powerful enough to help you make high-quality decisions and keep things on track, yet simple enough so you don't get bogged down in the minutiae. It lacks the detail, functionality, size, and/or scope of the original, but is representative enough that it can serve as a useful aid in understanding and decision making. Mental models can act like a bridge between technical and nontechnical people.

A good mental model captures high-level *reasons* for the more detailed technical processes. In business, those are usually reasons like cost containment, feature enhancement, and revenue growth. One way to think of this is that a good technical model describes *how*, while a good mental model describes *why*. This quality makes the mental model very good at helping you quickly understand important implications and also stay focused on the business reasons for your technical efforts.

"The first thing I did was sit down in a room with someone who knew the construction process inside and out, and was good at making spreadsheets," said Lee about how he approached his huge cell site construction challenge. He then began to build a mental model of how cell sites were built. "We worked at it all day, and by the end I understood that there were eighty-three steps to build a cell site. I also understood that there were a few things that absolutely needed to change if we were going to make it work. As a result, we knew exactly where we had to focus."

This is the process that Lee used to model a complex construction process in a little more than eight hours that could take years of on-the-job training to fully grasp. You can use it to build just about any mental model and convert something that you don't understand to something you can understand, work with, contribute to, and even innovate. In Lee's case, he was interviewing a technical person who understood the process that Lee wanted to model. While this is the fastest way to build a mental model, you can also use your own research and even trial and error to build and refine mental models. Here's how:

1. Begin at the End

A popular technique for teaching young artists how to sketch facial features accurately is to turn the image and the paper upside down. This shuts off the part of your brain that is interpreting what you *expect to see*: eyes, a nose, lips, etc. It then makes room for you to see and reproduce *what's actually there* in the form of raw shapes, lines, shades, and colors. The resulting sketches are always much more lifelike than their right-side-up counterparts. Starting at the end result and working backward when building a mental model has a similar effect. It allows you to let go of any preconceived ideas about how something *should* work and allows you to learn how it *does* work. Depending on what you are modeling, the end result might be the successful completion of a project, or a system's output, such as an engine's horsepower or the product of a chemical reaction.

2. Discover the Processes, Inputs, and Outputs

The first question Lee asked—beginning at the end—was something like "Okay, let's assume it's the first day of operation for a *completed* cell site. Tell me what had to happen right before that." He then listened to the answer, dividing what he heard into three parts: processes, inputs, and outputs. Keeping these parts straight is crucial for building an effective mental model, but to do that well, you only need to know the difference between nouns (people, places, things) and verbs (actions). Inputs and outputs are always nouns. Processes are always verbs. When the technician working with Lee said something like, "Then we have to get the drawings from the architect and submit them to the City," Lee heard this:

- **Process:** Architect *makes* drawings
- **Output:** Completed drawings
- **Process:** *Assemble* and *submit* paperwork for City
- **Output:** Submission receipt from City

This mental division may seem overly cumbersome at first, but it allows you to visualize and draw your mental model and later to work with the model to improve it. Models that mix outputs, inputs, and processes together are inflexible and difficult to understand—eliminating the benefits of creating the model in the first place.

3. Draw Boxes and Lines

To draw a mental model, put the processes in boxes and connect the boxes using lines for inputs and outputs. Here is an example of a very simple process drawn this way:

MENTAL MODEL: SANDWICHES

This "Sandwiches" mental model has only three steps, and represents the technical understanding of sandwich making that you'd expect in a young child. Imagine that child using it to explain to a younger sibling how sandwiches work. You can imagine the questions the younger child might ask when presented with this model. "Where do you buy the groceries?" "How do you know what ingredients to buy?" "How long does it take to make the sandwich?" "What are the steps that go into making a sandwich?" These are exactly the kinds of questions you should ask to expand and clarify your model. For each process that you don't fully understand, ask the following questions:

a. "What resources (time, money, etc.) are consumed by this process?"

b. "Is anything else required (inputs) for this process to work?"

c. "How do I know the inputs are sufficient for a successful process?"

d. "What are the outputs of this process?"

e. "What are the risks of the process not creating the desired outputs?"

Keep asking these questions until you understand the process completely, noting the answers in your drawing using boxes and lines. Notes about resources required can go in the boxes with the processes, and notes about the criteria and risks for inputs and outputs can go near the lines.

4. Get the Chunk Size Right

The chunk size of your mental model is the level of abstraction that you are using to describe your model. The smaller the chunk size, the more detailed, the more complex, and the more technical. It is best to start with a model that's too general, and then break larger boxes (processes) into smaller chunks with their own sets of inputs and outputs. Simply ask, "Are there processes that, taken together, make up this process?" For example, you could break the "Buy Groceries" process in the Sandwiches model into three parts: "Determine Ingredients," "Find Ingredients at Store," and "Purchase Ingredients." You *could* further break down the "Purchase Ingredients" process into smaller steps, and then further into even smaller and smaller steps. But there will be a point when you understand what you are modeling well enough to participate in a technical discussion and make decisions that reflect technical understanding. Other than for fun, there's no reason to get more detailed than that. Note:

Knowing that you *could* continue this process indefinitely to gain a more and more detailed and highly technical understanding of just about anything should feel empowering—even when you choose not to. All it takes is applying this set of questions to a source of information that spans a range of levels of abstraction for you to become a technical expert in just about anything. It's like a roadmap for how to invest in any technical skill.

5. Focus on the Critical Path (Remove Everything Extra)

After capturing all the processes, inputs, and outputs, go back and remove any process from your mental model that doesn't lead directly to the outcome that interests you. The step of removing extraneous processes is so powerful, it alone can spur paradigm-changing innovation. The "1-Click Ordering" button, for example, which reduced a seven-step process to one step, is one of Amazon's most significant patented innovations in the field of e-commerce—thought to be responsible for billions of dollars in additional revenue. Just as the innovators at Amazon did, look hard for anything extra in your mental model and remove it. In this diagram, the critical path is black, and the extra is gray.

CRITICAL PATH

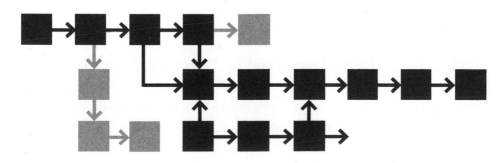

At about eight p.m. on the first day of their new assignment, Lee had just finished his mental model, but he was about to learn what he describes as "one of the most valuable lessons of my career." On his way out of the office, he ran into Dan, who, come to think of it, he hadn't seen all day.

"Where have you been?" asked Lee, curious.

"I've been out buying cell sites. Six so far," Dan replied.

This threw Lee for a loop, because—according to his brand-new mental model—buying the cell site was step sixteen, not step one!

"Wait a minute," Lee said, showing off his newfound technical understanding, "Don't we need the engineers to do a radio frequency analysis first to tell us where the sites need to be?"

"Well," Dan replied coolly, "I just drove up to the tallest building I could find and stood on the roof. You can't see everything, but looking around at the tallest points in town you can pretty well guess where at least six sites should be. So I bought them."

What Lee learned that day is that mental models aren't all built in conference rooms, on whiteboards, or in computer spreadsheets. Some people are more comfortable *learning* in order to *do*. Others are more comfortable *doing* in order to *learn*. And the best way to reduce redundancy and discover the true critical path is to use both approaches at once, which means that practicing the less comfortable method for you is a wise investment.

6. Challenge Assumptions About Resources and Prerequisites

This is your chance, as a nontechnical person, to add value to the technical discussion. People who are educated or trained in a technical field were taught a specific way of doing things, which is optimized to take advantage of all the beliefs and assumptions about the field at that time. As new discoveries appear in the field, new technologies and methodologies start to shift these beliefs and assumptions. Sometimes the state of the art in a given field changes so fundamentally that it renders the conventional way of doing things obsolete. In these cases, a technical person's training can actually become a liability and your technical ignorance can be an asset. To gracefully challenge someone more knowledgeable than you, ask questions like:

a. "What would we have to give up if we wanted that process to take a lot less time, money, or resources?"

b. "Is there any way this process could proceed without all of those inputs?"

c. "Is anyone else doing it differently?"

d. "What alternative processes were dismissed and why?"

e. "What would happen if we removed this step entirely?"

f. "What happens if we are willing to remove one of the criteria?" (Such as quality checks, longevity, scalability, repeatability, frugality, etc.)

g. "What happens if we had to do it in one tenth the time? Or for one tenth the money?"

Questions like these led to innovative solutions for Lee and his team. "We did a lot of things to shortcut the process. We built cell sites in the back of trucks and parked them on the street where the site should be while we waited for city permits to turn them on. We got the city to preapprove cell sites providing that we made them 100 percent safe and 100 percent invisible—something that had never been done before because the client had just treated the city's processes as unchangeable. That led to buying huge fake palm trees and hiding the cell towers inside. We approached one building owner [in a key location] with a drawing of a beautiful-looking clock tower [big enough to hide a cell site inside] on the top of his building and offered to build it for him at no cost. We even rented out a hotel room downtown and built a cell site right inside the room. I'm pretty sure no one had ever done that before." Challenging conventional wisdom made all of these ideas and their crucial time savings possible. This is the stage where the extra work of drawing the model correctly really pays off. The beauty of a good model is that it actually gives you good data when you play with it, and once you "teach" it the most accurate real constraints you can, it can "teach" you the most efficient and effective way forward.

7. Visualize Yourself Walking Through the Process

When you've completed your mental model, visualize yourself walking through it, taking each action, producing each output, and receiving each input. Don't rush this part. This is how you know you actually *understand* what you are modeling. Allow for your intuition to suggest that you might be oversimplifying or overcomplicating it. Trust your thoughts and feelings about it. When you can visualize each step vividly, understanding why it's there and how it relates to the other steps, you've successfully converted something "too technical" for you to understand into something you cannot only understand, but contribute to.

This is the blueprint for investing in your earning potential and capability of adding value to others through your technical skills.

To start building your own mental models, discard the idea that you are not technical and therefore are somehow deficient in your ability to understand how something works. You have the *capacity* to understand nearly anything, if you take the time to break it down into small enough chunks. That's exactly what Lee did in 1998 in order to build those cell sites.

With so much at stake, and with such a daunting task, you can just imagine the amount of monetary value that J. Whalen Associates might have captured when they finished the final site. "The amazing thing was we finished the twenty-eighth site at 11:55 p.m. on the last day of the deadline, exactly six months after that first meeting."

"MAKE IT UP ON VOLUME": RISK-REDUCING TECHNICAL SUPER SKILLS—FINANCIAL MODELS AND SYSTEMS THINKING

Use mental models to learn *enough* about just about any technical skill in a fraction of the time—starting with the other Technical Super Skills. If you are serious about learning to read, you have to start with knowledge of the fundamental building block of language: the alphabet. If you are serious about learning to increase your earning potential, you have to start with the fundamental building blocks of business: finance.

With a good text like Lawrence Tuller's relatively easy read *Finance for Non-Financial Managers*, you can model how finance works and learn some of the key vocabulary terms. Once you are familiar with the basics, fifth-grade math and a little common sense can help you understand the financial health of a project, product, or business. While financial literacy never made anyone rich by itself, financial ignorance has certainly claimed its share of fortunes.

Go a little deeper with a book like John Tjia's *Building Financial Models* and you can start to draw mental models using numbers and formulas instead of boxes and lines. *Financial modeling* is creating a picture (usually of the future) that de-scribes the financial impact of nonfinancial events. You can build financial models to answer questions like "Is it better (for the airline) to charge a few dollars for baggage or to add a few dollars to the airline ticket price?" "How many hours can I afford to spend on this project before I start losing money in the long run?" "How much commission pay can we offer our new sales VP next year?" Unless you plan on going into investment banking, a modest investment (think hours or days) in financial modeling will be sufficient to reduce your risk of accidently investing in broken ideas. If you can choose a few variables (like price, quantity, etc.), open up a spreadsheet program and create a formula that describes their relationship to one another (knowing when to add, subtract, multiply, and divide), and then you have the ability to guess how much money you'll need to start your first business or to show your boss how much she can expect to save by putting in place your cost-reduction proposal.

With a book like Donella H. Meadows's *Thinking in Systems* and a notepad to draw out your mental model, you could gain a practical understanding of the Technical Super Skill of *systemic thinking*—including a deeper understanding of how systemic thinking informs Systemic Spending, the Happiness Exchange Rate, tribe, and other key ideas in this book. Add systemic thinking, as described throughout the above chapters, to financial modeling and you can start to use these Technical Super Skills together to create surprising new solutions to difficult business problems.

Systemic thinking looks for leverage points that have a positive net effect on an entire system's ability to function rather than just a positive local effect. When you add interrelated factors to your financial model, such as your own happiness (the ultimate goal of your personal finances) or your health (both an outcome and an influence on the quality of input to your personal finances), you are likely to come to radically different conclusions. It is the marriage of these technical risk-reducing skills that gives rise to the most original new strategies and the biggest opportunities for you to bring new value to others.

THE MOST PROFITABLE TECHNICAL SUPER SKILL:
THE MARKETING CRANK

Perhaps the highest-leverage way to provide value and increase your earning potential—not to mention to increase the value of all your other skills—is to understand the basic things a business can do to attract more customers. Even though it is one of the most fundamental aspects of business, many people still treat it like a modern form of magic. In fact, searching Amazon for "Marketing Magic" turns up 119 matching results.

If you asked a sample of one hundred CEOs and one hundred entrepreneurs what they most want, we would guess 80 percent or more of them would report some version of "more customers" or "increased sales." If you asked that same group if they knew exactly what to do about it, we would guess at least 80 percent or more would admit that they don't.

How is that possible? There are a few factors working against them. First, it's hard to know what works for other companies. It's rare to get an inside look at someone else's marketing mechanisms. When you click on a sponsored listing in Google, you don't see the split testing, dynamic automation, keyword optimizing, cookie tracking, heat mapping, behavioral profiling, psychographic matching, or any of the other mechanisms influencing what you're likely to see and click on next.

Second, most marketing we have ever been exposed to as consumers is *brand* marketing—which has the objective of changing how you feel about a company. If a brand is the collection of associations, feelings, and conclusions that you make when you hear the name of a company, then brand marketing is the company's way of influencing those feelings. In the long run, those feelings do translate into buying decisions at the mall or the auto dealership, but influencing your immediate buying decision is not the goal of brand marketing. The kind of marketing that attracts new customers in the short term is called *direct* marketing. While world-class brands like Nike and Apple get far more value from their brands than they ever could from direct marketing, most businesses' brand value is an insignificant part of their financial strategy. They badly need to attract buying customers directly. Confused business owners often want their *direct* marketing to look and feel as good as Nike's *brand* marketing.

With this poor understanding of the underlying forces that shape direct marketing, most unsophisticated marketers just end up trying to copy what they have heard works for other people, and superstitiously cling to anything that produces a positive result. Hence, marketing "magic." This mass confusion and superstition about marketing represents a powerful investment opportunity.

Understanding the science of direct marketing removes the veil of magic and replaces it with predictable and foreseeable business outcomes. It also frees you from having to use methods of questionable taste that damage your brand (think huge red block letters, flashing arrows, and cable access car lot commercials featuring the proprietor wearing a monkey suit), because you understand what actually works for your audience. The most profitable Technical Super Skill is the ability to set up a direct *marketing crank*—a mechanism for attracting new customers to any business. If sales is the Super Skill of converting people who *know about* your company to people who are *paying customers* of your company, then direct marketing is the Super

Skill of getting potential buyers who *don't* know about your company to learn about it in the most favorable and inviting way possible.

You may think you don't need to learn about direct marketing if you aren't an entrepreneur or don't directly work in the marketing department of your company. You would be wrong. Direct marketing is the ability to get someone to take an action, in writing. If you're sending a group e-mail out to thirty people in your company, and you want them to open it, and then do something about it, then you need to understand direct marketing.

To invest in this Super Skill, follow blogs like Dean Jackson's *I Love Marketing*, Scott Stratten's *UnMarketing*, or the blogs associated with reputable marketing software companies like Marketo or HubSpot. You will likely get tremendous value out of following just about any marketing expert who seems to be familiar with your industry and whose style feels good to you. (These blogs and hundreds more can be found with a simple online search.) But in order to coalesce all those great mind-sets and ideas into a technical understanding of direct marketing, you'll need to understand the basic framework of how a marketing crank functions.

Bryan and Jennifer, his partner in life, business, and love, coined the phrase *marketing crank* while teaching thousands of entrepreneurs how to grow their businesses in online and offline courses and mastermind programs. A physical crank has a linear effort/output curve, which means that you have to turn it harder or faster if you want more out of it. Marketing cranks work the same way. If you put more effort, time, or money into a marketing crank, you'll get more qualified customer leads attracted to your business. If you let go of the handle and coast for a while, then the flow of new people at your proverbial front door will dwindle in kind.

This highlights a common error that most new entrepreneurs

make. Word of mouth is important—in fact, it's the primary source of new potential customers, or *leads*, for a majority of small businesses. It's a signal that your products or services are high quality, because people like them enough to recommend them to their friends. But—and here's the error—it isn't usually enough to grow your business. Word of mouth, at least the way that it's most often practiced, doesn't qualify as a marketing crank. It's very difficult to manually double the number of word-of-mouth leads a business receives (assuming that, as for the vast majority of businesses, your word of mouth isn't the result of a calculated customer loyalty program or viral loop built into the design of your product). If you can't manually double the "output" by doubling your "input," then the fate of your business is not in your own hands, and you are leaving your financial future up to luck, or at the very least up to someone other than yourself.

A true marketing crank is made up of three components that must work together: the *clear story,* the *assets*, and the *offers*. Understand these three components and you'll have the beginnings of a technical understanding of direct marketing.

THE MARKETING CRANK: **Part 1, the Clear Story**

The *clear story* is the narrative that explains why a customer should buy your product. It places firmly in the customer's mind four key statements:

1. You think . . .
2. But really . . .
3. And if you just . . .
4. Then you'll get . . .

Without a compelling story, your product is forgettable.

It's hard to imagine a more boring and difficult product to try to market than insurance. But one very large company, paired with a very small spokesperson, created one of the most effective (and expensive) campaigns in insurance history. American insurance giant GEICO reportedly spends roughly $1 billion a year so that you'll remember the phrase "15 minutes could save you 15% or more on car insurance." Most of its ads feature an animated gecko (meant to help you remember the name *GEICO*) looking straight into the camera and telling the same basic story.

Here's GEICO's clear story, paraphrased: "*You think* that changing insurance companies is a hassle that takes a lot of time and effort, and you'll just end up with basically the same rate. *But really* we've figured out how to give you a competitive quote in just fifteen minutes. *And if you just* take a moment out of your day and give us a call, *then you'll get* hundreds of dollars in spending money and basically the same insurance coverage you have now." GEICO's annual advertising budget breaks industry records year after year, which is probably because—boosted by an effective clear story—its analysis shows that its ads work.

Whether the *clear story* is explicit or not, and whether it's backed by a billion-dollar advertising budget or simply indicated in the header of your $347 Web site, it is essential to help customers understand *why* they should buy your product *now*. It's so powerful that if a potential customer was thinking what you claim in the *you think* statement, and if they are able to believe what you claim in the *but really* statement, they are very likely to take the exact action outlined in the *and if you just* statement—provided they want the benefit you promise with *then you'll get*. Get the formula right and it will be easy for you to create offers and build assets that attract new customers. Get it wrong and no amount of compelling writing, salesmanship, media buying, discounting, or shouting from the rooftops will draw a crowd of buyers.

THE MARKETING CRANK: Part 2, the Assets

If the marketing crank is a machine that predictably and repeatedly generates new customers, the *assets* are the cogs in that machine. They are the tangible elements of your marketing system, like e-mail subscriber lists, Facebook ads, or online sales pages. If the clear story describes *why* a customer might be interested in your product, the assets describe *how* a customer can express that interest and eventually be directed to make the purchase. The assets must fit together like gears in a mechanical device so that each is connected to the next in a logical flow. There are seven different types of assets in every marketing crank, and they always work in the same order. To help you visualize this flow, we've provided a simple mental model:

MARKETING CRANK: ASSETS

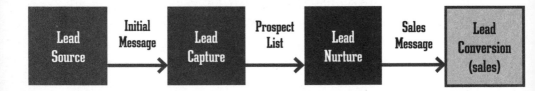

1. LEAD SOURCE. If direct marketing is like fishing, then the lead source is the lake into which you are dipping your line. This is a (large) group of people whom you can reach with your initial message. A lead source could be Facebook users, cable TV subscribers, everyone living in the 94116 zip code, bus passengers, your friends, or any group defined by a particular method of reaching them. It's different from a demographic like "men who play soccer" because a demographic doesn't inherently contain a way of reaching the individuals in the group en masse. A good lead source contains plenty of *reachable* people like your target demographic, and an affordable way to put your initial message in front of many of them at once.

2. INITIAL MESSAGE. In direct marketing, this is the money shot. It's the headline in a Google or Facebook ad, the subject line and content of a marketing e-mail, or the "call to action" on the radio: "Call now if you . . ." It's an explicit request for the customer to take a specific next step. Your initial message will be informed by the clear story but likely not reveal it entirely. With the ability to reach millions or even tens of millions of viewers (through channels such as social media platforms, television advertising, or online search engines), the difference between an initial message that captures 1 percent of its intended audience and a slightly better one that captures 1.1 percent can represent hundreds of thousands of additional prospects. Because the effects are so highly leveraged, Creative Super Skills like copywriting can be incredibly well compensated when applied to initial messages, with top copywriters often demanding fees up to $100,000 for a single-page initial message. Most initial messages in small businesses, however, underperform badly. They are often treated like an afterthought, applying little or no technical marketing skills—another great opportunity for the committed self-investor.

3. LEAD CAPTURE. The lead capture asset is the backbone of direct marketing, and usually completely absent from brand marketing. It's the process of recording a potential customer's contact information and getting their permission to contact them further. (Don't ever contact potential prospects without their permission, even if you happen to have their contact information. That's spam! It's unsavory, illegal, and for all but the most committed criminal spammers, totally ineffective.) While passing around a sign-up sheet at a seminar or scooping up business cards at a business convention are technically lead capture processes, by far the most effective is a Web-based system that asks people to subscribe to a mailing list in exchange for something free and valuable, making them your *prospects*.

4. PROSPECT LIST. Many entrepreneurs believe that a prospect list is a business's most valuable asset. It can be traded, bartered, leveraged, an even sold. To fully utilize its value, remember that this list is made up of human beings, and each person on the list has a very personal relationship to you, your brand, or your company. If you neither neglect them nor pester them, your prospect list will indeed become your most valuable business asset.

5. LEAD NURTURE. Direct marketing is like dating. Some people have the experience of love at first sight and know right away that they belong together. Most don't. The lead nurture process is the sequence of touch points that allows a customer to go on a few "dates" with you before it gets too serious—to become familiar enough with you, your company, and your products and services to be ready for a sales message. When you nurture your leads, you teach them your clear story, demonstrate your credibility, and foster the mind-set that the prospect is going to need in order to understand the value and significance of your sales message when you are ready to expose that to them. Some products—like disruptive technology products—require significant education before a customer can even begin to evaluate if they want to buy. Everything involved in this education process is included in the lead nurture asset. This process could look like a "drip campaign" of e-mails that are automatically sent every few days, a series of invitations to view demonstrations or free online Webinars, or if you are doing business with a more archaic company, even a weekly round of golf. You may casually present a few sales messages along the way during the lead nurture process, and when a prospect responds to one of them, you're one step closer to gaining a new customer. Friend and Internet marketing expert Eben Pagan has taught nearly a million entrepreneurs to "move the free line," which means investing so much in lead nurture that you give away valuable products that would ordinarily cost hundreds or thousands of dollars, just to maintain a positive relationship. Counterintuitively, people who have received a lot of value for free don't walk away with a full belly—they have an even greater appetite to buy from you, because they trust the quality of the products and services you offer.

6. SALES MESSAGE. This is the invitation to have a "sales conversation" with you about the problem your customer wants to solve and whether they'd like to use your product or service to solve their problem. This "conversation" might take place in the form of words on a shopping cart page on your Web site, or a conversation with a friendly employee in the dressing room of a retail store, or a series of meetings between the executives of two large companies. The more high-touch your sales process, the more likely the initial message simply gauges the customer's interest in having a dialogue. The more low-touch (like an online sales page or a retail checkout counter), the more you rely on the initial message to close the deal. If the rest of the assets in the marketing crank are high performing, fit together well, and powerfully evoke the clear story, then pressure on the sales message is actually quite low. As long as you don't introduce any new doubts, inconsistencies, or barriers for the customer at this point, a healthy percentage of people who participate in your lead nurture process are likely to become candidates for lead conversion and pay good money for your products and services.

7. LEAD CONVERSION (SALES). We drew this box in white in our mental model above to signify that it's really a sales process and not a marketing process, but we've included it here to show how the two work together like a relay race. This is where your marketing crank hands the baton to your sales team (even if you are also the only member of that team, as is the case with businesses that you run by yourself). Also, many businesses have completely touchless or automated sales processes (like most online retailers or consumer packaged goods companies), meaning that the "salesmanship" has to be accomplished by the marketing crank because there's no opportunity to answer last-minute questions or address last-minute objections. If this last step—the process that converts leads into customers—is done person to person, then its success depends on the Interpersonal Super Skill of sales—outlined in chapter 3—and not a technical skill like direct marketing.

THE MARKETING CRANK: **Part 3, the Offer**

Whereas the assets describe *how* a customer learns about your product or service, and the clear story describes *why*, the *offer* defines exactly *what* they're buying. The more compelling the offer, the less precise the clear story and assets have to be in order to reliably attract new customers. Of the three, the offer is probably the most studied and the best understood by executives and entrepreneurs, but too many still lack a technical understanding of how an offer really works. A "solid offer" is made up of four parts, commonly referred to as "The 4 P's of Marketing." The secret to coming up with good business ideas is to keep talking to potential customers, iterating, guessing, and testing, until you have an idea that can answer the following questions with simple, powerful answers.

1. PEOPLE. Who is the product for? Great offers are specific about who can benefit. The Hard Rock Hotel & Casino in Las Vegas uses magazine ads that feature pictures of businesspeople with partially exposed tattoos and piercings. The caption, "You know who you are," speaks right to their target market: professionals who have left behind a rebellious past.

The *P* for *people* also asks the question "What is special about the people who are making the offer?" All other things being equal, it's a much better offer to get basketball lessons from an NBA star than from a librarian. Be clear about the credibility of the people making the offer, even if it's not your main selling point. In the age of social media and viral marketing, *people* make a bigger difference than ever in the power of your offer.

2. PROMISE. What problem or opportunity is the customer trying to address? To what extent will this product or service help the customer address it? (Note that realistic claims almost always outperform suspiciously grandiose claims.) The more credible the offer, and the more of a bull's-eye for a need that the customer *already knew they had*, the better.

Don't fall into the trap of making your offer too creative, clever, or transformational. Unless you've got the creative ideas and financial backing of the late Steve Jobs, stick to what the customers already know they want. You can open their minds to new possibilities *after* they've signed on the dotted line.

3. PROCESS. What is the form in which the promise will be delivered? Is it a large appliance delivered to your home? Is it an online subscription service? Is it hands-on, like a massage or dental work? Is it one-on-one consulting? The process usually describes both the buying process and the process of using the product or service. Oddly enough, the process often has a bigger impact on price than the promise does. You'd expect to pay more for a bad concert than a great movie—because the process of delivery indicates a different value, even if the great movie promises a lot more entertainment. You can use this to your advantage: if your customers are pushing back on price, try changing the process to one of higher perceived value.

4. PRICE. How much will the customer pay? This might, for complex goods like a car, include a calculation of the total cost of ownership, which could include maintenance, insurance, fees, and other add-ons. In some offers, the price is the centerpiece of conveying the value of the offer: "Three payments of only $29.95!" In others, the price is the least significant factor in the value of the offer: "Get your car washed in the parking lot while you're at work."

Getting customer feedback is essential to building and refining a good offer, but unless your customer is giving you feedback in the form of actually making a purchase, what your customer tells you about price is almost never reliable. The bottom line is that they *just don't know* what they would pay until they are actually in the position of having to make a purchase decision. Set a price that allows for a comfortable profit, high enough to give you room to invest in enhancing the product over time, and low enough to make the final sales offer a no-brainer for the customer.

When the clear story, assets, and offer are all in sync with one another, a business that puts effort into its marketing crank will have a constantly flowing source of new customers. Sometimes business growth comes from investing more effort into an existing marketing crank. Sometimes it comes from investing in layering multiple marketing cranks together in a cooperative system. Either way, a technical understanding of the forces that drive direct marketing takes the magic and mystery out of how to grow just about any business. This is why it's important for every employee of a business to understand the main marketing cranks fueling the company.

Understanding how the marketing cranks work can reveal to you which projects and teams are most vital, and most strategic. Let's say you work in the finance department and you have the chance to work on one of two projects. One is to estimate the cost of a potential change in benefits provider over the next five years. The other is to give the sales department a tool to estimate the impact of discounted pricing on deals they are working on. Your peers might not see it, but all other things being equal, the latter project—simply because price is connected to the business's marketing crank—is likely going to end up being seen as a more vital project to the leadership. If you want to maximize the speed of your career growth within almost any company, get yourself assigned to vital and strategic projects and then make them work because you "get" technical skills, like how the marketing crank works.

The marketing crank is so fundamental to business and yet so rarely understood, and such a significant opportunity to provide value, it is essentially its own "business in a box." With a modest self-investment, you could likely create a $100,000-plus per year consulting practice just by applying this model to small- and medium-sized businesses in your geographic area, provided you've invested in some of the Interpersonal and Creative Super Skills required to sell your services, develop compelling stories, and lead your clients to adopt your way of thinking. If you already are a bright strategic thinker, effective leader, creative storyteller, or one-to-one salesperson, this Technical Super Skill could easily help you follow in the footsteps of so many others, and be the basis of a consulting practice that easily reaches six figures per year and beyond.

CHAPTER 6

INVEST IN PHYSICAL SUPER SKILLS

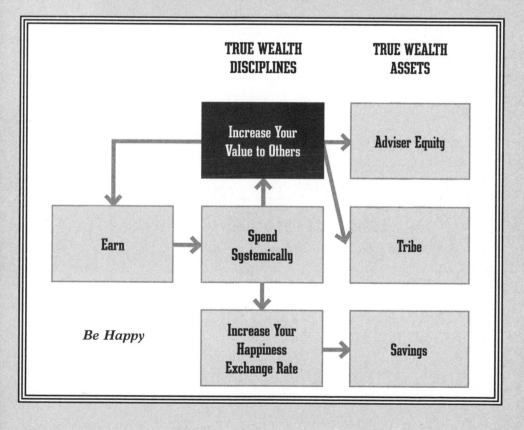

- LONGEVITY
- MENTAL FOCUS
- CLEAN, HEALTHY APPEARANCE
- CLEAN, ORGANIZED ENVIRONMENT
- HEALTHY RELATIONSHIP WITH ALCOHOL/DRUGS
- GREAT SEX

The day after Valentine's Day, 2009, forty-seven-year-old Steve Cooksey asked his wife to take him to urgent care. His health had been declining for months—"I felt terrible all the time. Lethargic, no energy, sluggish, horrible mood. It got to the point where I could barely get myself out of bed." He collapsed the moment he got to urgent care, and they put him in a wheelchair. Suspecting the symptoms of diabetes, they took his blood sugar reading. It was at 740 mg/dl, which is off the charts. (A normal range, at fasting level, is around 80-130.) They rushed him in an ambulance to the emergency room.

Steve passed out a few times in the ER, and the doctor told him he was on the verge of a full-blown diabetic coma, a medical emergency that can be fatal. They kept him in ICU for four days with IVs stuck in him before they could get his blood sugar down to a safe level.

"My lifestyle up until that point, in one phrase, was 'sedentary sloth,'" Steve said. "My normal breakfast was going to Bojangles' Chicken 'n Biscuits and getting a couple of biscuits with their sweet tea and Bo-tato Rounds [hash browns]. Then I'd go out to lunch, and I'd get breads and rolls and buns and I'd eat spaghetti. If I wanted to eat 'healthy' I'd get a big-ass salad, but I'd use the sugary salad dressing. If we went to fast food, I'd get a big Subway sub, with juice or Gatorade or Pepsi. My lunches were full of carbs. For dinner, I'd stop and eat a Big Mac or a Big Fish sandwich, with French fries and sweet teas. I was feeding that carb addiction sixteen hours a day. At my peak I was around 235 pounds [at a height of 5'10"]—and that was not muscle, it was mostly flab."

As they let him out of the hospital, the nurse gave him a

copy of the Food Pyramid to put in his pocket, and told him to keep his eating below 2,200 calories. That was the only dietary advice any medical professional at the hospital gave him, after he nearly died.

"When I heard that, I thought, 'That's basically like I eat now!' I could still eat bread and cookies and drink juice on the diet they were recommending to me." Instead of rejoicing at this freedom, Steve smelled something fishy. He intuitively felt that there must be some link between all the sugar and carbs he was eating, and his blood sugar issues, even though the hospital doctors did not mention such a link. He began looking into the matter.

Steve's general practitioner suggested that some diabetic patients were having success with a low-glycemic diet. Cooksey bought *The New Glucose Revolution* by Dr. Jennie Brand-Miller, Dr. Thomas M. S. Wolever, Kaye Foster-Powell, and Dr. Stephen Colagiuri and started following its low-carb prescription. "Very soon, I needed less and less insulin. By the end of March I was off all the drugs they had put me on in the hospital. They had told me I was going to be on a lot of these for the rest of my life, but I refused to believe that. Just a month later, I was off cholesterol drugs, I was off blood pressure drugs, I was off diabetes drugs, and I was off insulin."

Impressed with the power of this simple dietary change, he began learning more about low-carb diets. He discovered the blog of Mark Sisson (www.MarksDailyApple.com), author of *The Primal Blueprint*. Sisson's book and blog are central resources in a subculture of low-carb eating called "Paleo," which encourages followers to focus on foods that were originally available in our ancestral environment, such as meats, fruits, and vegetables, and to avoid recent additions to the human diet, such as grains, legumes, and of course refined sugar.

Cooksey dove headlong into Paleo, and adopted this lifestyle and philosophy as a central part of his life. "I've been on a rocket ever since. I'm fifty-two years old. I'm in the best shape of my life." Steve recently weighed in at 165 pounds, having lost around 70 pounds since his day in the hospital. Like many Paleo enthusiasts, he's embraced the trend of barefoot running—and recently completed a challenge of one hundred barefoot miles in thirty days. Steve now devotes himself to writing a blog called Diabetes-Warrior.net, which is one of the top sites on the Web providing Paleo information for people with diabetes.

Had Steve listened to what the hospital doctors told him, which was their best attempt to summarize the results of well-established, widespread health studies and experiments, he'd still be eating the Food Pyramid way, and he'd probably still be overweight and stuck on meds.

Instead, Steve Cooksey decided to go searching for a map to his own "hidden treasure." Right now, out there in the world, there are hundreds, perhaps thousands of what we call hidden treasures within your life: opportunities and changes that will take you to the next level, if you discover them. To find these hidden treasures, you need treasure maps. These are small pieces of information that will have a large impact on your life, if you follow them. For Steve, a major treasure map in his life consisted of these three words: "Eat low glycemic." Had he not found that map and followed it, his life would be radically poorer. He might not even be alive.

A Super Skill is a skill that benefits *all* areas of your professional and business life, leading to higher earnings. (Super Skills also tend to be very beneficial to your Happiness Exchange Rate, as they make your work much more enjoyable, turning work into a source of pleasure instead of pain.) Physical Super Skills are those that relate to what might be called the *personal operating system* of your own business life: your body and brain;

your health and vitality; fitness, sleep, and energy levels; and your focus, mental capacity, and concentration.

It is important to note here that we are not talking about Physical Market Skills. Physical Market Skills such as craftsmanship or skilled manual labor can be traded on directly (albeit rarely for very high compensation). Physical Super Skills as discussed in this chapter only rarely make you money directly. They do, however, greatly contribute to the intangible factors—confidence, presence, trust, energy, charisma, motivation—that often determine your ability to take advantage of potential earning opportunities, and that increase your Happiness Exchange Rate. They also increase your longevity, allowing you to stay in the game of life actively for a longer period, earning more money, creating more value, and making a bigger impact. Last, and perhaps most important, like all Super Skills, these physical skills increase the value of and marketability of *every other skill you possess.*

While this may not be a complete list, it represents all of the most common Physical Super Skills that have both a reliable systemic benefit when you invest in them and a reliable path for investing in yourself with a very high likelihood of success. We've omitted any would-be Super Skills that require any special traits or advantages not found in an average person, or that have investment requirements outside the reach of an average person.

INVEST IN INCREASING THE LENGTH OF YOUR PRODUCTIVE WORK LIFE

One of the most direct ways to invest in your earning power is to invest in increasing the length of your productive work life.

While no one can say definitively what steps to take to do so, here are some commonsense suggestions that seem highly likely to pay off in this regard:

- Get yourself in great cardiovascular shape.
- Obtain your ideal, healthy body weight.
- Eat less sugar and processed junk food, and more whole grains and fresh fruits and vegetables. As Michael Pollan writes in *In Defense of Food*, "Eat food. Not too much. Mostly plants."[1]
- Quit smoking, overdrinking, and any other addictive use of drugs.
- Get enough sleep.
- Work reasonable hours, with plenty of time for recreation and play.
- Find a spiritual practice that is meaningful to you.
- Seek help and healing for emotional and psychological troubles and disturbances. (This goes for all of us.)
- Develop a rich, nourishing web of ties with friends and family.

Our guess is, if you've read this list, you may be thinking, "Thanks for the advice, buddy! And how the hell do I do all of *these*?!"

This is not an all-purpose self-help book. Obviously, we cannot give advice on how to solve all of these problems and achieve all of these goals in the space of one book, nor do we have the credibility and expertise on all of these issues to do so.

Our point is a broader one: *these are worthy things to invest in.* They are worthy not just because they will enrich the experience of your life through an increased Happiness Exchange Rate and increased internal wealth (though they will). They are also worthy as investments in the cold, harsh calculation of dollars and cents. Because most of these things (particularly if taken together systemically) will likely lead to a great *quantity* and *quality* of productive work life. That is, you'll be able to remain productive for more years, and your productivity (due to increased focus, energy, mood, etc.) will be higher throughout.

If you are earning $100,000 per year around normal retirement age, and all of the changes above allow you to extend your productive working life happily and zestfully for five additional years, you've just brought $500,000 in additional earnings into your life. Potential returns like that justify significant investment, as much as or more than any stock, bond, mutual fund, 401(k), or home equity.

The problem is, because their returns cannot be quantified exactly, investment advisers and gurus do not recommend these areas. If a financial adviser is handling your portfolio, and the stocks she has chosen rise 10 percent, she knows (a) that *her* choices led to that result, (b) exactly what the result was, and therefore (c) exactly what her reward or compensation will be, based on any contractually specified management fees. Without precise quantification, there is no compensation.

If she was instead to recommend investing your money into cooking classes in order to eat more healthily at home, for example, she wouldn't know (a) whether that recommendation led to any financial gains at all, (b) if so, exactly what those gains were and how much could be attributed to this investment recommendation, and therefore (c) there's no way she could get compensated for such a recommendation.

No compensation, no recommendation. That's how it works with traditional financial advisers. And that's why you don't hear them talking about the kinds of investments we talk about in this book.

That doesn't mean they're not good investments. It just means they're not amenable to standard investment analysis.

Is there any doubt that Steve Cooksey, who was at death's door, gained tremendous earning power throughout the (newly increased) length of his life, and with the newfound energy and vitality he can apply to his work now? For Steve, the investment of time, effort, and money it took for him to learn to eat Paleo was an investment with a return simply unavailable through traditional financial investments, in terms of both external and internal wealth.

INVEST IN IMPROVING THE QUALITY OF YOUR MENTAL FOCUS AND PRODUCTIVITY AT WORK

This is a huge issue in the knowledge economy. With corporate employees sending and receiving an estimated average of 125 e-mails per day,[2] demands on attention are increasing steadily in most work environments, to what some might consider levels that reach absurdity.

Take two people who have roughly the same educational credentials, and roughly the same training, technical knowledge, and background.

One of them has fantastic attention and just gets down to work. She has a clear mind, is focused, and can get right to work and not be distracted for long periods of time. She goes through the day with a great level of energy and focus and attention.

Compare that with your typical corporate worker, who is drinking three or four cups of coffee just to wake up in the morning and get started. Her attention wanes throughout the day, and she is distracted by all manner of attention lures on the Web, not to mention watercooler banter and chitchat.

Comparing these two people, who is going to win in her

career? The first person, ten times out of ten. The first person will probably also report an increased sense of power, efficacy, and satisfaction at work, leading to a higher Happiness Exchange Rate.

In economics, productivity is conceived of as labor multiplied by capital. The amount of labor you can bring to a day is fixed—probably around eight hours per day. Ten to twelve hours at the very most, on a sustainable basis. Therefore, the way to increase your productivity is through increasing the capital you are mixing with that labor. One of the most powerful forces of human capital you can attain is the power of your focused attention.

You can invest in your attention by studying a productivity system that works for you, such as *Getting Things Done* by David Allen or *Master Your Workday Now!* by Michael Linenberger.

You can also invest in your attention by studying meditation or mindfulness. Michael, who has practiced meditation a great deal himself, has developed his own take on traditional mindfulness practices, stripped of any spiritual mumbo-jumbo, and offers a complete course in meditation for free at Immer siveAwareness.com. If you would like something in person, you can search online for "mindfulness" or "meditation" classes in your area; in most cities you'll find numerous options, from the most secular to the most mystical and spiritual.

When there is a premium on peak performance, such as toward the end of an important project; right before a big meeting, pitch, or public talk; or in the midst of a big deadline; investing in massage, private yoga sessions, acupuncture, or a trip to the spa can yield very large systemic returns. These are what we would call *high-leverage* periods of time, where performance increases of 5 to 10 percent can yield a huge difference in the outcome of your earnings or performance that year.

Few books would recommend a massage as a serious invest-ment; this book is the exception. Michael has consistently found that a ninety-minute massage, costing around $150, increases his mental focus, concentration, and calm for several days. If those days happen to be leading up to a big public talk, pitch, or writing deadline, $150 for a major performance boost at a criti-cal point is about the best bargain we can think of. There is a fair amount of cultural programming, surrounding the idea that slowing down, de-stressing, and taking care of your body are luxurious, unnecessary "indulgences." You must overcome this cultural programming in order to engage in and benefit from these kind of investments, but once you do, in times of acute stress and needed peak performance, "indulgent" investments in de-stressing can have surprisingly large returns, in higher performance and earnings.

A whole different rabbit hole you can go down, if looking to invest in your calm, focus, and mental energy throughout the day, is nutritional supplementation. We are not experts in this field, so we can't make specific recommendations. However, there is a whole field called "nootropics" you can look up online, having to do with legal, cognitive-enhancing nutritional supple-mentation. Another great resource to start with is the book *The UltraMind Solution: Fix Your Broken Brain by Healing Your Body First* by Mark Hyman, MD.

We think the best way to invest in your mental focus and attention is via self-experimenting with which kinds of diet, ex-ercise, and sleep patterns give you the most consistent energy and focus throughout the day, via the self-experimentation guidelines offered in chapter 3. It's not in the scope of this book to tell you exactly *how* to bring this result into your life, but rather, to motivate you to *invest* in finding the best method that does bring this result about for you.

INVEST IN MAINTAINING A CLEAN, HEALTHY PHYSICAL APPEARANCE

There is a substantial cultural bias benefiting people who are more attractive. Attractive people are more often hired and promoted, and less often laid off. According to *The Wall Street Journal*, "Attractive people are likely to earn an average of 3% to 4% more than a person with below-average looks. That adds up to $230,000 more over a lifetime for the typical good-looking person."[3]

You might think this unfair, if you hold on to the assumption that physical appearance is a trait that you are born with and can't do anything about. Nothing could be further from the truth. According to *Business Insider*, "You don't have to hit the genetic lottery to become more attractive. . . . Thanks to a slew of studies on sex and attraction . . . [there are simple things you can do] that are proven to make you more appealing."[4] Basic hygiene, smiling more, wearing clothes that fit, and eating more vegetables (proven to give your skin a natural glow) are just a few things you can do to start giving yourself an edge.

When you look better, you feel better about yourself. Feeling better about yourself gives you confidence, which in turn makes you appear more attractive. Regardless of your physical starting point, investing in the belief that you are—or at least can be when you choose to be—an attractive person is an essential part of any serious self-investment plan. If you don't believe you can be attractive, then you don't *try* to look attractive, and then you aren't.

Your investment can range from fifteen minutes of vigorous dancing in the morning in your bedroom to tens of thousands of dollars for a brand-new wardrobe, personal stylist, personal trainer, weight-loss coach, and therapist to develop better habits and remove any residual limiting beliefs.

Different people will experience vastly different returns on investment in this area. If you are already fit, slim, and attractive by conventional standards, and/or if you already know how to present yourself attractively through fashion and wardrobe, you are probably already in the zone of diminishing returns for further investment in this area. However, if you have carried around that "extra fifteen pounds" for most of your life, or if you put little attention into your self-presentation via fashion, wardrobe, grooming, and styling, you are probably in the zone of increasing returns on investment in this area, and might find very large systemic returns for reasonable amounts of investment here.

In many tech companies in Silicon Valley, for example, there is a casual, anything-goes attitude toward style and self-presentation at work. However, just because you *can* show up to work unshaven in a hoodie and shorts doesn't mean you *should*. We all have a superficial side, and to imagine that the people who have influence over your career (including your customers, if you're in business) are not making superficial judgments about you, based on appearance, is to assume too much.

Potential avenues of investment include quality hair styling, wardrobe and style consultation, fitness training, hiring a nutritionist or personal chef for better eating at home, and even psychotherapy to overcome persistent negative body image.

We recommend investing a little bit more here if you already pay attention to your physical appearance in a professional context, and investing a lot more here if you have been ignoring this aspect of your life, or if you've had the attitude that it shouldn't matter because people should just love you for the work you do.

MAINTAIN A CLEAN, ORGANIZED ENVIRONMENT

Customers and coworkers tend to assume that the state of your work environment is a reflection of your state of mind. If you work collaboratively, people will be more enthusiastic about working by your side if you keep your environment organized. Organized people tend to keep more promises and feel less stressed than those who are less organized. Most messy people think they are messy because of their personality type or because they like it that way, but usually they are just lacking a few organizational systems. Hiring an organizational consultant to put a few systems in place (like a simple system for sorting and filing mail in your home) or hiring a maid to straighten up a couple times each month can be an ultra-high-leverage investment without requiring you to change any substantial personal habits.

The self-amplifying aspect of investment is evident here. If you already have a critical mass of earnings, spending systemically here yields a much larger result. For example, it is reasonable to assume that an upgrade in the organization and orderliness of your physical work environment could increase productivity by 5 percent. A 5 percent edge in productivity, year after year, is much larger when you are earning $250,000 per year than when you are earning $25,000 per year. The returns on investment increase as your earnings increase, allowing you to cycle back more of the earnings into increased investment in other areas of your life, in an upward spiral.

DEVELOP A HEALTHY RELATIONSHIP WITH ALCOHOL AND OTHER SUBSTANCES

We're not here to preach about how much alcohol you should drink, or what other substances (licit and illicit) you should consume or not consume. However, we will note that the value of external and internal wealth that has been utterly destroyed from an out-of-balance relationship with alcohol and other drugs (including death from tobacco use) must total in the hundreds of trillions of dollars. Few things will derail your productivity in your career, and will cause your internal wealth to tank, faster than a serious imbalance in this area.

Thus, getting (or keeping) a grip on your use of alcohol and other drugs is a powerful systemic investment in your earning power and your Happiness Exchange Rate. We are not here to tell you how to do this. However, we would like to point out that there are a number of options available now beyond the traditional twelve-step model (which many people are uncomfortable with, due either to its religious overtones, its "once an addict always an addict" belief, or the seemingly unrealistic admonition to cut substances out of one's life entirely, forever). If you are alienated from the traditional models for any reason, a good place to start looking is the book *Rational Recovery* by Jack Trimpey.

GREAT SEX: DEVELOP A RELATIONSHIP TO SEXUALITY THAT IS EMPOWERING AND LIBERATING

When planning your career and thinking *linearly* about how to invest in your own ability to be valuable to other people, it would be ridiculous to put having great sex on your agenda. What could your sex life possibly have to do with your work life? Conventional wisdom is to keep these two worlds as separate as possible, like a city's sewer system and its water supply. But as you learn to think about your life *systemically*, including your earning potential, your financial security, your spending, and your investing, you'll begin to see that few areas of your life have a greater global impact on your motivation and vitality than a great sex life. In turn, motivation and vitality are precious personal resources in the pursuit of being valuable to other people.

As a reminder, a shortcut to systemic thinking is to observe how changes in one area affect *every other* area or context in the system. Through experimentation, both of us discovered in our own private sex lives what has been known to many people for thousands of years but is still a radical idea in a corporate setting: as humans, our sexuality is deeply tied to our creativity and motivation. The systemic effect we each observe in our own lives of putting attention on having an empowering and liberating relationship to sex is an increase of creative fuel and a more powerful presence, activating Creative and Interpersonal Super Skills.

We've not only seen this relationship between sexual liberation and/or empowerment and professional prowess in our own lives, we've also incorporated this understanding into the professional and executive coaching advice we each have given—and in our tiny sample of hundreds of clients, we observe a reliable correlation between a healthy sex life and a healthy work life.

To begin to understand how this could be, let's take a step back and define more specifically what we mean by *great sex*. A healthy relationship to sexuality is both empowering and liberating. *Empowering* here means that you feel powerful in the domain of sexuality. Feeling sexually powerful means that you have a sense of control over your own experience, that you can bring as much or as little sexual "charge" to an interaction as you choose. That no one else but you can decide how turned on you feel, and that you have access to creating in your own body the sensations you choose to have when in a sexual relationship.

Liberating means that you experience progressively more freedom to think about sex and sexuality as much or as little as you wish. A sexually liberated person is fluent with their own desires and feels no shame or wrongness about any desire that may well up inside them, even if they decide not to act on that desire in order to preserve other values. They have no bounds or arrested attention—neither on aspects of sexuality they wish to avoid nor on obsessive thoughts of aspects of sexuality they wish to experience.

To fully understand how great sex can systemically impact your other Physical, Creative, and Interpersonal Super Skills, it's important to consider what the impediments to great sex are. What are the factors that might *decrease* empowerment and liberation? They are the exact same factors that might decrease your confidence, presence, and self-esteem at work: *self-judgment, shame, low self-esteem, a belief that something is wrong with you, lack of trust in your inherent value and beauty.* Collectively, we call these factors "repression" of your self.

If you are getting the idea that what we mean by great sex might not be what's typically portrayed in the media or by some overly objectified, airbrushed lingerie model, you are on the right track. A great sex life, by our standards, is not about quantity, availability, or ease. It's an inner journey to unearth your own pockets of self-judgment, shame, and unhealthy external biases and heal them with a loving partner (or partners) who celebrate you fully as a sexual being.

How would one go about investing in becoming a better lover? Whether you're single or in a relationship, the basic method is much the same. The key is to treat your own sexuality as the greatest art form in which you will ever participate—an art form you plan to cultivate your entire life.

Great sex of course requires learning skills. There are hundreds of books, workshops, and even online courses now in which you can learn every skill possible, from the most subtle forms of sensuous massage, to the most exalted spiritual techniques of Tantra, to the naughtiest rope bondage. A simple Web search should turn up dozens of courses in any major metropolitan area.

But this art form goes way beyond techniques. Ultimately, the best artist is the one who puts the most of herself into her art. Commit to investing time (and this investment of time should be the most fun in the book) to putting *all* of yourself into your sexuality. You're probably already used to putting the tender, loving side of yourself into your sexuality. What would it mean to put, for example, your sense of creativity into your sexuality? Your sense of spirituality? Your sense of humor? Your intellect? These are all things that, with discussion and play, you can explore with your partner or lover.

But even that doesn't represent *all* of you. The greatest art expresses more than just the sunny, happy, joyous sides of life. What would it mean to express your sense of sadness, or even grief, in your sexuality? Your anger? Your hopes for a better world? The more of yourself you can express in your sexuality, the less compartmentalized it becomes, and the more it becomes an expression of your deepest and fullest self. A true art form. In fact, the only art form that nearly *every* human has the capacity to master.

CHAPTER 7

ADVISER EQUITY

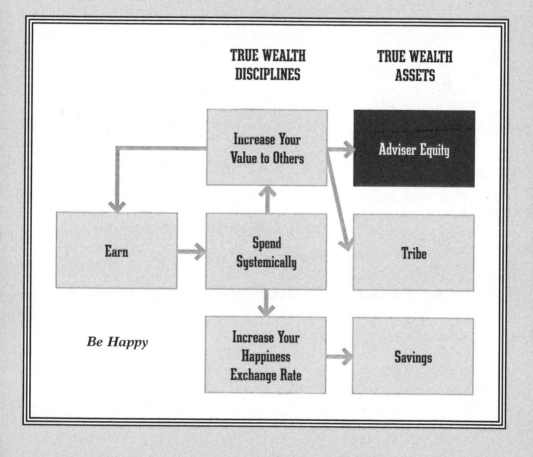

- SHATTERING THE RULES OF FAIR COMPENSATION -
- HOW AVERAGE PEOPLE CAN MAKE EXCELLENT ADVISERS -
- SYSTEMIC AMPLIFICATION -
- HOW TO KNOW WHAT WILL GROW -
- THE WEALTHY LIFESTYLE, EVEN WITHOUT THE WEALTH -

A woman living in a trailer park made twenty years' salary in one day working as a secretary.[1]

A consultant with no formal training and no high school diploma earned $18,750 per hour to talk with employees.

A man from New Jersey earned $26 million working as a cafeteria chef.[2]

Craig Silverstein, a software engineer, earned more than $800 million by age thirty-seven.[3] (This is 8,600+ times the average annual pay for software engineers.)

David Choe made an estimated $500 million from (legally) spray-painting the inside of a single building.[4]

If these true stories seem like they shouldn't be possible, it's because the rules of workplace value exchange—which say you should only expect "honest pay for an honest day's work"—have brainwashed you into thinking they aren't possible.

You may never have been taught these rules explicitly, but chances are you've learned them all too well. You probably believe at some level that bosses *should* make more money than their employees. That working harder *should* make you more successful. That more responsibility at work *should* mean longer hours. That older people (with more tenure) *should* make more than younger people. That other people doing similar work *should* be paid the same as you. And that what you earn in life is based on what other people who have more power than you (like employers, customers, or bankers) agree to give you.

These rules may seem like they are made of concrete, but there is one instrument that is powerful enough to break through and crack them apart, like the roots of a tree slowly buckling a residential sidewalk.

This root system, for capitalism, is *equity*. Though equity—or business ownership—is virtually worthless at the beginning of a company's life, it is powerful enough to cross the boundaries that govern compensation, making millionaires out of secretaries and CEOs out of college dropouts. If you acquire it before it becomes commoditized or "securitized" on the open markets—a process that strips it of its unique power—equity has the ability to help you escape the traditional structures of compensation. It invites you to have a hand in building something great, and to receive rewards based on the greatness of what has been built, rather than the effort it took to accomplish the building.

Equity gets its power from the sheer scale of impact that a company can have in today's global economy. Broadly, one way to estimate the value of a company is to calculate the potential value it can deliver to customers. Generally, companies that can reach a vast audience with a relatively small incremental cost tend to be the most valuable, which is one reason most of the best-known rags-to-riches stories come out of the tech sector. As technology advances, reaching more people becomes cheaper and easier, and equity becomes *more* powerful.

When the value of your creation is suddenly a thousand times greater than the effort you put into making it, all but the greediest of people feel they have more than they need. Most people reach a sense of sufficiency when they stand to receive even 50 times the value they expended, leaving 950 times the original value available if it expanded a thousand-fold. That newly created value has nowhere to go except to everyone you can think of who helped you—even slightly—along the way. Equity is the vehicle to distribute this "excess" value. This is how Silicon Valley massage therapists, graffiti artists, secretaries, and parking attendants end up earning millions.

Texting company WhatsApp proved that 55 people can build a Web-based company that reaches 450 million users in just a few years. When founders Jan Koum and Brian Acton sold the company, buyer Facebook valued what they had built at $19 billion (a few billion more than technology company Seagate, a more typical company in that price range). Seagate took ten times as long to reach its current value—about forty-three years—and required roughly 52,100 employees to run instead of only 55.[5] We're sure many of those employees work just as hard, are just as creative, and just as clever as the team from WhatsApp. But the value of what they've built, when divided by the effort it took, is only 0.001 percent as much. That pretty much leaves the concrete "rules" ground into dust.

The trailer park secretary, known as the "Netscape Mom," was paid partially in equity ownership (in the form of pre-IPO stock) in the company. The day Netscape went public, in 1995, her stock was suddenly worth more than a million dollars. David Choe is the graffiti artist who turned down $60,000 cash to spray-paint murals at the corporate headquarters of a young company—opting to be paid in equity instead. Smart move, because the unknown start-up turned out to be Facebook and his equity turned out to be worth half a billion dollars.

The uneducated consultant agreed to reduce her fee by thousands of dollars for just over ninety hours of work in exchange for equity that was worth roughly $1.8 million a few years later. Silverstein and the New Jersey chef both earned their fortunes working for (and receiving equity in) Google.

Because of the absurdity of the numbers, it would be understandable to make the mistake that most people do: to think of people with stories like these in the same category as lottery winners or the recipients of huge punitive damages awards. To assume their fortune is based *solely* on luck. It isn't.

Choe was pretty lucky that he chose to paint the walls at Facebook instead of any of the dozens of social networks that have come and gone. But he and each of the others earned their equity by providing meaningful value to the companies. Most agreed to take a risk by forgoing some cash in favor of becoming a part of the company's root system. Were these five equity earners lucky? Yes. Were they *just* lucky? No.

Perhaps more important to the equity story than these five lucky outliers is the far more common positive results that lie in the middle of the equity pack. People who are actively engaged in working for equity do their best to pick good companies. Of course they are hoping for the big win. And while there are certainly thousands of inspiring stories of people converting equity into a multi- or even a hundred-million-dollar payday, there are also *millions* of stories of people turning equity into a multi- or even a hundred-*thousand*-dollar payday. A solid base hit. An estimated 14.7 million Americans have participated in employee stock ownership plans in recent years,[6] and the vast majority earned at least some positive gains.

Bryan has seen many prudent equity workers turn their equity into a six-figure score within three years—especially if they add value to a company that's been in business for about two years and has more than fifty employees. Do this repeatedly over the course of a career and you could become a wise shopper of potential employers in much the same way that A-list venture firms like Sequoia Capital and Greylock Partners have honed their ability to pick winning teams and products, making a big "exit" (opportunity to trade your equity for cash) seem less and less like luck.

This practice is common enough that some executives in the Valley refer to equity shoppers who haven't yet had their first big exit as having "dodged the wealth bullet." The exaggerated implication is that all you need to do to get rich in Silicon Valley is to stand still long enough.

But the SAFE plan doesn't call for you to move to Palo Alto (the heart of Silicon Valley) and become a pre-IPO equity shopper. It calls for you to invest in developing something that shares the rule-destroying power of equity but in most other respects behaves completely differently: *adviser equity.*

The first step in bringing the wealth-building power of adviser equity into your life is to understand what it's not. It's not making the cover of *Wired* with your new hot tech start-up that you thought of in the shower. It's not participating in the employee stock purchase plan as employee number 2,300 either. It's not striking it rich with your iPhone app idea. It's not using your 401(k) to buy your company's stock with its "matching" program. It's not even being employee number 3 at Google (Silverstein) or working eighty-hour weeks as a secretary until you wake up a millionaire one day (Netscape Mom).

These are the most visible equity stories, representing the extreme ends of the spectrum of equity holders, but they aren't the most common. As ideas, they may be popular, but they don't make for much financial security.

THE INVISIBLE MIDDLE

Probably the most romantic character in American business is the inventor. We love the story: the inventor becomes the founder, who becomes the CEO, who becomes the billionaire. But it's so unlikely for us to reach a similar destination, even if we dedicate our lives to replicating their footsteps in every last detail. Most of the time, when a person believes in a future vision that no one else does, it's because that future isn't going to happen.

Most truly original ideas are unique because they are uniquely *bad* ideas. Contemporaries thought these heroic inventors and their "bad ideas" were crazy at first because, in a very real way, they *were* crazy. They believed in something that was real only for them and no one else—then staked everything on the idea that they were right and everyone else was wrong. On the other side of the coin, many desperate and destitute inventors believe—citing the experience of their heroes—that blind conviction alone is evidence enough that they are destined to succeed. "No one believed Nikola Tesla either!" Statistically, this is a very bad bet. You have but one life, with perhaps a handful of decades to apply toward creating value in the world, say five. Given that it usually takes one to two decades to see a greatly innovative company mature into an unbridled financial success, how many bad ideas can you afford to pursue?

Inventors and founders are at the tippy top of the equity scale when it comes to the size of the personal windfall accompanying their company's IPO or acquisition. The instances of these "bad ideas" turning out to be brilliant ideas in disguise are rare, but when they do happen, the payoffs are enormous—which is what makes the top end of the scale so highly visible.

But notice that each of the extraordinary examples at the beginning of this chapter relies on doing *ordinary* work in exchange for equity: assisting, consulting, cooking, programming, and painting. Not extraordinary inventors' work like predicting in advance that VHS will beat Betamax or foretelling the next revolution in digital music distribution. This is to illustrate that enormous payoffs—though still very rare—are not reserved for our romanticized inventors, founders, and CEOs at the top end. In fact, far more wealth is made helping other people bring their ideas to fruition than will ever be made developing a new idea from scratch.

Your best chance of developing adviser equity is to heavily invest in the skills that are both interesting to you and useful, then offer these skills to people who you believe will be successful in the future. With almost 28 million small businesses creating 65 percent of the new jobs in the United States, and more than 500,000 new businesses started each month, there is likely a very rich market for skills relevant to business success within driving distance of your home.[7] Surely all of these new businesses have at least two things in common: 1) they badly need expertise and labor relevant to making them successful, and 2) they badly need to conserve cash. These are the ideal conditions for anyone interested in acquiring adviser equity.

Once you begin to master an important skill that enhances your value to others (especially if you invest in the Super Skills prioritized by the SAFE plan in previous chapters), find people who need your skill but are too early-stage in their projects or companies to be able to afford to pay you market rate in cash. Just as our five lucky earners did, forgo some or all of a typical cash payment in exchange for an interest in the future of the project. That interest, be it formal or informal, is adviser equity. Any one of the Super Skills could be the basis of an effective adviser equity asset, though probably advice about sales, marketing, copywriting, and Web development would be the lowest-hanging fruit. It doesn't have to be a Super Skill. It could be anything of value to others—even improving employee morale by spray-painting a fantastic set of murals as Choe did.

The most common and basic form of this kind of help is advice, hence the name *adviser equity*. But just about any service can be exchanged for equity, and all equity gained in this kind of exchange qualifies as adviser. It is even possible to earn adviser equity in an individual—provided they have the means and the impetus to share the tangible benefits of their future success with you.

The defining characteristics are: 1) your influence increases the likelihood of a future positive outcome, and 2) you have an expectation to share in the benefit of that positive future. Notice we are careful not to say "money." Equity is often realized in cash, but adviser equity can be realized in any form that is valuable and meaningful to you. (Michael has a permanent invitation to a very unique and highly exclusive series of parties near New York City, which would be impossible for almost anyone else to attend, as a result of the adviser equity he earned from giving advice, and making connections, for the host. He values this far more than cash he might have received for advising the host.)

We don't mean to discourage you from playing at the top end of the equity scale, following your dream and starting a company. In fact, we personally love the idea of your investing in your original inventions and unique ideas. Just like we personally love the idea of your going salsa dancing or scuba diving on the Great Barrier Reef. Part of True Wealth is having the freedom to follow your passions, and if you have done the work that this book suggests, you will undoubtedly find passion in developing new ideas that contribute value to others. But if this happens to take the form of an innovative company with untested technology or an unproven marketplace, we strongly suggest that you invest only time and money you can afford to lose, because while it *could* have a positive impact on your financial future or even a multimillion-dollar payday, it can't form the backbone of a legitimately SAFE financial plan.

In fact, if you have a passion to invent something new or create a radically innovative company, let that burning desire be even more motivation to build the True Wealth assets of tribe, savings, and adviser equity so that you can buy yourself the runway to give your idea the best possible chance of taking off. Your True Wealth assets can give you the time you need to get your innovative idea or start-up off the ground, and can give you the perspective you need to make grounded decisions about your invention or innovation. Just don't confuse the statistically microscopic probability of an enormous outcome with a SAFE plan for your financial future.

Whether because of an overreaction to fear of failure or

because of prudent wisdom, the majority of the millions of formal equity holders fall into a psychological trap at the *other* end of the scale, aiming too low rather than too high, as employees with insignificant amounts of stock with insignificant upside. By the time a company has created a formal "stock purchase plan" administered by the human resources department to hundreds and hundreds of employees, chances are all the power that equity could contain has been sucked out of the offer and it is either far too diluted or far too late in the growth story of the company.

Also on the bottom end of the equity spectrum is your ownership in your own small lifestyle business. Some of the businesses that Bryan and Michael own are consulting businesses, and though they provide plenty of income and opportunity to provide value to interesting clients in a manner consistent with what matters most to us, there is virtually no way to convert this ownership into other forms of value. We can't "sell" our businesses without selling ourselves along with them, because they would have no value to anyone but us. There are many reasons that it may be beneficial to "own your own business," including possible tax advantages, flexibility with schedule, and the freedom to determine your own destiny. But *equity* isn't one of them. A good rule of thumb is this: if you wouldn't buy someone else's business of the same type as yours, then it's pretty likely that no one would buy yours either. If there are no buyers, usually there's no "exit."

Between these two extremes is what we call the *invisible middle* in adviser equity. Invisible because no one would be interested in the unspectacular newspaper headline "Friend Cashes In $94,800 in Equity for Sound Advice When Company Sells for $18 Million." No one except perhaps the one receiving the check. Invisible because getting help and giving away a portion of your company are personal matters—likely to be left out of your Twitter feed. It would be odd to send out a tweet proclaiming "Needed help firing key employee, gave 1% of co to @fred for the assist!" Without news or social media coverage, unless you are directly involved in an adviser equity deal, it's very unlikely you'd ever hear about it. And invisible because a representative from Human Resources will never sit down with you and go through a nicely designed packet of information explaining to you how it works.

Consider this your packet.

━━━━━━━━━━

If you use your skills to benefit other people's success, from time to time they will want to express their gratitude by giving you something of value. If you help them a lot, and they succeed a lot, then that something might include formalized equity in their future concern. These agreements form your adviser equity and can be formal or informal, explicit or implied.

Gratitude is the engine that makes adviser equity work. That means it's very unlikely for you to negotiate your adviser equity up front.

Todd Hopkins and Ray Hilbert, inspired by real conversations with overqualified applicants for a janitorial position, wrote the book *The Janitor: How an Unexpected Friendship Transformed a CEO and His Company*. The parable highlights a late-working CEO's conversations with the Janitor as their paths cross each night. The Janitor doesn't know much about running a company, but the universal lessons that he lives his own life by prove to be sound guidance for the business leader.

Imagine if—as soon as their first conversation began—the Janitor had stopped the discourse to negotiate the terms of his adviser equity. It would surely be the end of the conversation. If you are not already receiving abundant gratitude, then regardless of how highly you value your own advice, it doesn't warrant and is unlikely to garner adviser equity. Now instead imagine that the CEO goes on to successfully sell the company, and his gratitude for the Janitor is overflowing because he knows that he would never have been able to do it without the sage wisdom he received in his nightly conversations. If the CEO's own personal benefit from the sale was a modest $3 million, could you imagine $30,000 or even $90,000 making its way to the Janitor? Up to three times his annual salary for essentially forming a friendship. We don't have to imagine it because this is exactly the kind of gesture that so many entrepreneurs are quietly benefiting from—including many millions of dollars of benefit to our friends, acquaintances, clients, and ourselves.

The story reminds Bryan of when he was first being paid to coach CEOs at the age of twenty-seven. Bryan wasn't a janitor, but he might as well have been. He didn't know much about the job of being a CEO of a start-up company, but he *loves* people and had run a small team of sound technicians in his previous role, so he knew a few things about how to maintain high-quality relationships and keep a group of people engaged in working toward an outcome. In 2000, with companies laying off record numbers of employees and being forced to rethink their business plans in the face of the tech bubble burst sometimes referred to as the "Dot-Bomb," maintaining good relationships with key employees and keeping teams focused on the task at hand became very important for CEOs. So important that they were willing to overlook the fact that they were learning how to do it from someone thirty years their junior.

This is the essence of adviser equity: a human friendship that allows you to transcend your roles and titles (ordinarily a CEO wouldn't take business advice from a janitor or someone as young and inexperienced as Bryan was at the time) and bring all of your life experience to bear on their situation, effectively enough to engender authentic gratitude.

Generosity and friendship are the basis of adviser equity. But don't expect your friends to spontaneously cut you in every time they experience a big win. A more typical sequence leading to adviser equity might be this: You help answer a question or two over lunch or at a dinner party. You offer to have a more in-depth discussion. Either at the conclusion of that discussion or after some of your advice has started to pay off, one of you suggests to the other that you make a slightly larger commitment to the future of their project or company. It's okay to be the one to suggest it. In fact, until you gain a reputation for being a great mentor for young entrepreneurs and businesspeople, it's likely you'll have to bring it up first. Talk about ownership percentage (if it's to be formal) and expectations about demands on your time. Half a percent for one meeting every three months is not uncommon, though larger percentages are appropriate for companies and projects that are higher risk or that have a less probable exit.

THE MISSING PIECE IS MORE VALUABLE THAN THE WHOLE PIE

Within a year of his first gig helping a CEO with his key employee relationships, Bryan saw a pattern develop. The number of viable companies surviving the Dot-Bomb was shrinking rapidly. To any CEO who wanted to take him up on it, Bryan made the following offer: "I'll work with you free for as long as it takes for you to get a great role as CEO of a company that you believe is going to thrive in the new [more challenging] environment. All I ask in return is that—provided it makes sense—you bring me into your new company as a coach and pay me with some combination of cash and stock." Even though he knew much less than they did, the nature of his work gave him more exposure to companies than they had. And when CEOs are looking for a job, that's what they most want.

For the handful of clients who took him up on his offer, Bryan went to work on helping them build great relationships with board members and investors (the people who hire CEOs) instead of with key employees. To Bryan it felt like very similar work, and his greatest risk was his time. In late 2001, he hadn't yet learned very much about how to be a good CEO but, for his clients, he held the key to a valuable missing piece: how to build great relationships. His well-timed offer was the beginning of building the adviser equity that eventually boosted his coaching and consulting practices to be among the most successful in the Bay Area.

To gain significant adviser equity, you'll want to be working with the highest-achieving people possible (whatever that means to you). They have the most at stake, their future is already probably pretty rosy, and your chance of participating in something truly great is much better. Most people get a little weird around "high-level" people. It's hard to make an offer for adviser equity when all you can think of is some version of "I'm crap! What can I possibly offer this successful person?"

But there's a counterintuitive secret about highly accomplished people. They tend to *need* less and *appreciate* more. In our experience, it's much easier to contribute to someone who feels smarter than we are than it is to help someone who's struggling with the basics. Take two people you'd like to invest in; we'll call them Moshe and Blake. For argument's sake, let's say what they both want is to be able to run a marathon. To make it fun, let's also imagine that you are not a runner. Blake is also not a runner. In fact, he's not in very good shape. He's drawn to work with you because he feels intimidated by other trainers who are too athletic and can't understand his penchant for fried food.

Moshe is a runner. He, in fact, has won several half marathons, but has a mental block about running the full twenty-six miles that he doesn't really understand. He's drawn to work with you because he overheard you telling a story to someone else about a mental block that you used to have about playing guitar in front of people.

At Moshe's urging, you walk him through the mental process you used to get over your mental block, replacing "guitar" with "running" as best you can. You can see his wheels spinning as he's trying to adapt your method. He asks you questions for clarification. Through the process, you are learning a little bit about running, and there is an unexpected similarity that you both discover about the two disciplines. You both talk about "the zone" and what it takes to get into it and stay in it. Moshe tells you that's basically the key to the marathon (from the perspective of someone with his physical abilities). You've paid a lot of attention to being in the zone when playing guitar in the past. So you list all the ways that you've learned to stay in the zone while playing guitar, including a cool trick your first guitar teacher taught you.

Meanwhile, you decide to spend some time with Blake. You share some of the insights about the zone that you learned with Moshe, but Blake just looks at you like a dog squinting into a fan. Blake's never experienced the zone so he really has no reference for it. His first question is "I've run three miles at once, but my knees really start hurting and I have to stop. What should I do?" That one stumps you, not really being a runner yourself, and you end up kind of staring awkwardly at each other.

Moshe is a high achiever. That means that he has only a few missing pieces to the puzzle (mental blocks and strategies to stay in the zone). Because he's already invested a great deal in all the other pieces of the puzzle, the value of that one piece is astronomical for him. He is highly likely to break the tape on the finish line at the next marathon he enters, and he is highly likely to be thinking of you with gratitude as he does. From his perspective, you are the difference between finish line and no finish line, even though from your perspective all you did was take a stab at applying some things you learned playing guitar.

Strangely, you were more able to provide value to Moshe with just the one missing piece than if you knew a lot more about running but lacked guitar experience. High-achievement people also tend to have the Creative Super Skill of context importing, so they can help you find what is useful to them by working in multiple contexts at once. This is why it's important to bring all your life experience to your investment in other people's success. You never know which piece of the puzzle will be worth the whole pie to them.

Your own self-image might try to fool you into thinking that you should help people who aren't very successful (and aren't likely to be very successful) because you have more confidence that they will look up to you in some manner. To help with your self-image, get in the habit of getting feedback about how much value you tend to provide at work, in your community or tribe, and with your closest friends. If you still lack confidence, put more energy into mastering the Super Skills, and trust that those skills contain missing pieces for even the highest-achieving people.

SYSTEMIC AMPLIFICATION OF YOUR VALUE AS AN ADVISER

You still might think that "all of your life experience" is hardly enough to improve the chances of anyone's success, much less a CEO's. That may be true for now. But this is one thing that the

FACD plan and the SAFE plan have in common: they both acknowledge that building valuable assets takes a series of baby steps over time. If you don't already have experience in business leadership, don't expect to transform into a full-time equity adviser overnight.

To put adviser equity and your specific ability to cultivate it in its proper context, we'll need to look at a typical investment time line, for both the SAFE and FACD plans. We've already discussed the FACD plan of devoting your teens and early adulthood to formal education, then entering the workforce and saving as aggressively as you can, investing these savings in financial investments that (supposedly) appreciate in value, until retirement day.

Of course it doesn't work, for reasons we've already discussed throughout the book, but that's what most financial "experts" continue to say is best.

SAFE Plan Investment Time Line

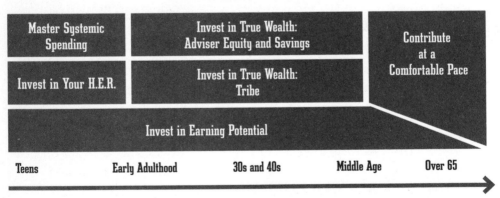

Now let's watch the SAFE plan unfold over time. Following the narrative as if it were an ideal life story, it might look like this: Through trial and error as a teenager, invest in your ability to master systemic spending. Over five to ten years, once you know how to systemically optimize your financial ecosystem to produce the kinds of outcomes you most want, gradually give way to investing in adviser equity and savings. At the beginning, your attempts to develop adviser equity might be dubious or even a flat waste of time. But at this stage, it's more about learning and detecting the best opportunities to provide value. To allow for some effortless savings, it's essential to get your Happiness Exchange Rate as favorable as possible, a priority investment younger in life. Very gradually, as you realize that what makes you happiest of all is spending time with people you truly love and admire, this investment in your H.E.R. gradually becomes your investment in your tribe.

Of course you start investing in your earning potential as early as you know what it means—perhaps even before your teens. You continually upgrade and enhance your ability to be valuable to others throughout your adult life, easing up only once you feel both the capacity and the desire to dial back your active engagement in contributing value to others. (Keep in mind that this desire might not manifest—the irony of the SAFE plan is that, when it is well executed, your financial capability to stop working increases as your desire to contribute value in the form of your work increases.)

Into your thirties, perhaps you focus on strengthening your most refined Super Skills. Perhaps you focus on raising the waterline by bringing up your worst skills to at least a minimum bar. By the time your investment in adviser equity has hit full swing in your late forties, you've had as many as twenty-five years of practice, increasing your value to others using Interpersonal, Creative, Physical, and Technical skills. That's enough to master a great deal of finesse and sophistication across several important contexts.

Your adviser equity opportunities grow rapidly, and your income grows rapidly, but with a healthy Happiness Exchange

Rate, your spending doesn't, leaving a larger and larger deposit in the savings account each month. As you round past middle age and find yourself turning sixty-five or seventy, you've gradually adjusted the kind of work you do to be more focused on providing benefits to the people you most love, your tribe. You've also replaced any aspect of the work you do that's too difficult or incompatible with your ideal later-in-life lifestyle with lower-effort/higher-leverage contributions (such as making introductions, and providing high-leverage advice over lunch). With that accomplished and a full complement of Super Skills to bring to bear on any collaborative effort that inspires you, you are well positioned to design your lifestyle any way that your Happiness Exchange Rate suggests. In short, you are happy and secure.

The self-amplifying nature of the plan hits a tipping point sometime in your thirties or forties, unlocking an especially powerful systemic effect between equity, tribe, and earning potential. This just scratches the surface, and we're sure that you can think of more examples of cross-amplification than we have space to print here, but understanding how these positive effects are interrelated is an important part of imagining how you will eventually acquire significant adviser equity:

1. EARNING POTENTIAL ENHANCES EQUITY. The greater your earning potential, the greater bargaining power you have when you want to forgo cash in favor of stock or other forms of equity. A copywriter who can demand $100,000 to produce a sales letter will earn a lot more adviser equity than a copywriter whose work is valued at only $1,000 by the marketplace. Greater earning potential also puts you in closer proximity to decision makers and business leaders, because they want to work with high-level people.

2. EARNING POTENTIAL ENHANCES TRIBE. The more income you have, the wider range of people you can easily consider peers. The more value you have to offer, the more at home you will feel with other people who have a lot of value to contribute. (Of course, there's a big difference between "has a lot of money" and "has a lot of value to contribute." Tribes of "value providers" are far more generous with one another than tribes made up of people who are wealthy but aren't giving or skillful with their time. Tribes that are overly focused on financial status tend to feel gross and shallow. When a friend is in need, often a person with a higher *earning potential* will have more ideas, resources, and abilities to help than a wealthier person with less value to offer.)

3. EQUITY ENHANCES EARNING POTENTIAL. The more people and companies whose future you are invested in (emotionally, financially, or both), the more varied the education you will get from working with them. Bryan is sought out by first-time CEOs to help them ensure success based on wisdom gained primarily by learning from his past CEO clients.

4. EQUITY ENHANCES TRIBE. Equity-related companies and projects tend to be tightly aligned with your values, as does your tribe. The more high-quality adviser equity assets you build, the more likely you can introduce your tribe to the people, projects, and companies that are most exciting for them. Matchmaking between an equity adviser project and a tribe member enhances both assets when it's authentically a good fit. In addition, most informal adviser equity—like a standing invitation to use box seats or Tom's ski boat from the introduction—is best enjoyed with friends, naturally enhancing your relationship with your tribe.

5. TRIBE ENHANCES EARNING POTENTIAL. The more awesome people you call your best friends, the more opportunity you will have to meet and work for the exact kind of company, person, or project that excites you most. As your tribe expands and more people find out about you by reputation (really just your good friends appreciating you on loudspeaker), getting new opportunities or resources to learn how to meet new challenges with excellence becomes easier and easier.

6. TRIBE ENHANCES EQUITY. Your first several adviser equity opportunities will likely come from your tribe, start as friendships that are aligned on values, and mature into business relationships in which you've taken ownership and accountability in the success of their future.

We can't overstate the power of systemic amplification. Instead of competing for your time and investment dollars the way the two different assets might in the FACD plan, these investments each enhance the value of all the others. It's this amplification that puts *adviser equity* within reach for the average person over time, even if he starts out with "nothing valuable to offer."

With the FACD plan, there's no way to start at fifty and "make it" for the typical American earner. Even with the "miracle" of compound interest, fifteen or even twenty years just isn't enough to buy you enough retirement time. With the SAFE plan, it is definitely *better* to start earlier, but there's no such thing as too late. A dedicated person with average intelligence and access to the Internet should be able to develop any one or two of the Super Skills in a powerful enough way to offer in exchange for adviser equity in no more than three years. Maybe even significantly less. Good progress on systemic spending and your H.E.R. is easily achieved in that same span of time.

Entrepreneurs, both the VC-funded variety and the bootstrapped, work-from-home type, likely have the greatest need for help with their futures, and also have the best supply of equity to offer (including revenue sharing, preferred stock, LLC membership, success fees, etc.). The shortest path to getting high financial returns from your SAFE plan is to focus on developing the Super Skills that you find they want most, even if they don't seem to relate at all to your current line of work. Again, sales, marketing, copywriting, and Web development seem to us to offer the highest direct tangible returns for the least time invested.

Unlike with your earning potential, there is nearly unlimited opportunity to earn adviser equity. There may only be a few "salesman" *jobs* available in your area at any given time, but every business will always welcome new sales. They may not want to hire someone, taking on the risk of paying their base salary and training them, but even a business that's not hiring is open to getting a little help or well-timed advice (especially for $0 up front).

Often equity opportunities are designed to convert to cash for you (or whatever tangible benefit you agreed upon) in a maximum of two to five years, so theoretically you could go from "absolute zero" to realizing greatly enhanced financial returns in as little as five years. That is, of course, if you can invest in the future of the *right* people and companies with your adviser equity.

CHOOSING THE RIGHT PEOPLE TO INVEST IN

Given our emphasis on directing your own financial destiny, it might cause you to raise an eyebrow that we don't count ownership in your own lifestyle business as the True Wealth asset of equity, but we do count a small percentage of ownership in other people's businesses—including lifestyle businesses. If you, yourself, are indeed the last safe investment, why isn't your company the best source of equity? Why choose to divert any time away from self-investment to invest in other people? Two reasons.

First, you have likely already captured almost all the value you can from your own business, given your current level of development as an entrepreneur. Despite what many entrepreneurs want to believe, business income tends to be limited by marketing, sales, and product *strategy, quality,* and *consistency,* and very rarely by *time, capital,* or *size of staff.* Spending twice as much time barking up the wrong tree won't produce twice as many cats. Diverting a couple hours each month from binge-watching the latest TV series to working on your business is therefore likely to produce very nominal results. Not to mention that you are already due 100 percent of the profit, so declaring some portion of that profit as "counting" toward equity gains you nothing.

Second, for adviser equity to play a meaningful role in your financial future, you have to mitigate the risk that some of your investments may become worthless. The most effective way to reduce that risk is diversification.

It's better to have 1 percent ownership in one hundred companies than 100 percent ownership in one of the companies in that group—even if you pick the one that appears to be lowest risk. This is what distinguishes *adviser equity* from its riskier cousin, *sweat equity.* Usually, to earn a significant amount of *sweat equity* (ownership interest awarded for the labor—the sweat—of the owners), you must devote a lot of your time to *sweating.*

If a partnership forms between a "silent" partner who puts in the money—*buying* equity—and someone who puts in the effort—for sweat equity—the "silent" partner expects the other to commit most of his available time to the project. If they get the impression you aren't solely focused on looking after their financial investment, they might stop being so "silent" and force a renegotiation of the partnership agreement. Compared with adviser equity, this time requirement (a contractual minimum of twenty to sixty hours per week is common) makes sweat equity very expensive.

Adviser equity is not free. It costs you *some* time. Once you've honed your ability to contribute to the success of others, your time costs should be less and less, but never zero. You don't have the capacity to invest in an unlimited amount of formal adviser equity—the kind that involves a signed document granting you some defined benefit such as ownership of stock or a percentage of future sales. In addition to your initial investment of time, these types of formal agreements usually come with a future time commitment on your part as well.

As we've said above, one ninety-minute meeting every three months is enough to earn formal adviser equity in most companies. Even that small amount of time, when multiplied by ten, twenty, or even thirty adviser equity investments, starts to feel like a significant use of attention, a resource that most people feel they have very little of to spare. In a landmark 1968 study, stock market analysts John L. Evans and Stephen H. Archer argued that you can achieve most of the risk-reducing benefit of diversification by investing in just ten companies. Later analysts found the point of diminishing returns (where the overhead of adding additional companies to your portfolio outweighs any benefit from additional diversification) to be around thirty stocks. Whichever the correct number, it is just a slice of the entire field of possible investments.[8]

Your time is limited, so you must get good at choosing the right people to invest in. To give you a head start, we will share with you the criteria that we use to guide our decisions about where we should acquire formal adviser equity in a business, based on the successes and failures of more than one hundred projects and companies that we've invested in. (Note that informal adviser equity—the kind that is based purely on friendship, gratitude, and reciprocity, which we discuss later in this chapter—may be more freely given, because it doesn't bind you to a formal time commitment in the future, and it doesn't pay to be strategic with your friendships. It is unfeeling and unloving to attempt to evaluate if a person is "worth" investing in as a human being. That answer is always yes. This, however, is the best information available on how to decide if a person's *business* is worth investing your valuable time in exchange for formal *adviser equity.*)

About Them . . .

1. SAY: DO. Pay attention to the ratio between what they say will happen and what does happen. Particularly when they have a direct influence over whether it will happen or not. If honesty is only promising what you intend to deliver, and integrity is doing everything you can to deliver on what you promised, Say:Do is honesty + integrity + wisdom about how unforeseen circumstances will likely affect what you can deliver. Don't waste your time investing with people who are chronically optimistic about the future, are repeatedly late on deadlines and commitments, or habitually hedge and "sandbag" (purposely underestimate their future results so they can appear to have perfect track records). People with high Say:Do ratios (high means they do what they say almost all the time—no one is perfect) tend to be more successful in everything they do, because their interface with other people is cleaner and they are operating with an accurate map of reality—allowing them to change course more quickly and precisely. We'll invest with someone who changes course effectively over someone with better credentials, an impressive résumé, or even someone who starts off on a much better course. Unless you are earning your *adviser equity* by running their business *for* them, they are going to have to put your advice into action in order for it to make a difference. People with low Say:Do ratios will find themselves stopped and not willing or able to muster the resources to work around their obstacles and implement your advice. No implementation, no results. No results, no success, gratitude, or equity value for you. It is *possible* for people to change their Say:Do ratio, but there's no reason for you to bet your future True Wealth on this being the moment in time when that will happen.

2. (JUST) BEFORE THEY RISE. Analyzing data from the 2012 U.S. Census will confirm what you might guess intuitively. Before age twenty-four or twenty-five, it's hard to tell the difference between a "late bloomer" and someone who will hug the bottom of the income scale for the rest of their life. Then, from age twenty-four until about forty-four, across every income segment, people in the United States experience the fastest income growth of their lives, with the highest income bracket making the highest percentage gains. Presumably this is because this is the period of greatest learning from work experience and the period when most people have the most energy and enthusiasm for work. Statistically, if you help a twenty-four-year-old with the key Super Skills they'll need to be successful, the income growth they are likely to experience from that success in the near future will be much greater than if you applied that same help to a fifty-four-year-old (or an eighteen-year-old). But the real x-factor isn't the person's age. It's whether or not they seem to you to be on an acceleration path with respect to their careers, their project, or their company.

3. THEY BELIEVE. Confidence doesn't ensure business success as an entrepreneur, but lack of confidence almost never accompanies it. Investigate their fears, doubts, and concerns. Having them is normal (and if they don't seem to have *any*, then that brings up a different concern!), but see if you get the feeling that they are going to allow their fear to stop them. It's important that they believe in themselves and in their product, but it's even more vital that they believe in their mission. A company's mission is its "why." If there is more than one person on their team, then alignment on the *why,* as well as the *what,* and *how,* is essential. For teams of five or more, in our experience, alignment is the best leading indicator of achievement. If you believe in only some of the team members or only some of the team members believe in the *why,* walking away is a good bet.

About You . . .

1. YOU BELIEVE. Don't talk yourself into anything. The gap between "I believe" and "I want to believe" is much larger than it feels. Do *you* believe in their mission? Do *you* believe their product or service will meet customer needs and serve their mission? Do *you* believe they have the skills and the motivation to make it work? New ideas can be seductive. Weed out the ones not worth investing in by asking yourself, "If my circumstances were different, would I be willing to work for this company full time?"

Make sure your belief is based on understanding the business and its customers, not on the conviction and reasoning of the people running the business. If it's too far outside your own direct experience, your ability to spot warning signs (not to mention offer meaningful help) will be hampered, and it may be better to pass.

2. THE MISSING PIECE. Make sure you can offer them an important missing piece. If they need to focus on manufacturing in China and your expertise is in Web design, this isn't likely a great opportunity for adviser equity for you. The missing piece shouldn't be money. As an adviser, you should be working almost exclusively with businesses that already have adequate funding. If an unfunded business is as good as it seems, it will find funding soon enough and you can invest in its success at that point. Let the sophisticated financiers figure out if it has a future.

About the Company . . .

1. THE CUSTOMERS BELIEVE. It's not enough for you and the business owner to believe in the product or service. The customers must believe in it too. Even the smartest equity investors in the world don't think they can outsmart customers. They look at customer "traction," or evidence of customers' investing real dollars in the product, service, or solution, to tell them how good an idea really is. Look for growth, response rate, and customer satisfaction rate.

2. MULTINODAL BUSINESS MODEL. This one's optional, but can be the most valuable: If you divide all the possible business models into two groups based on their basic method of value exchange with customers—binodal business models that do business directly with their customers and multinodal business models that set up a community between customers and charge some percentage of the value exchanged in the community—most of the fastest-growing companies in recent history will fall into the second group. Apple, eBay, PayPal, Facebook, Google, YouTube, and new darling WhatsApp all share multinodal models. As user networks grow, the company's profits grow exponentially.

About the Deal . . .

1. A MEANS OF EXIT. In order for adviser equity to add real value to your True Wealth, you must have some way of converting it to savings—or directly to the kinds of experiences you would ordinarily have to spend from savings to get. Just owning a percentage of a business is not enough. Owning a percentage of the business usually means getting paid when the business is sold and *not* participating in the profits along the way. If you want to earn formal adviser equity in a project or a business that isn't likely to be sold and you want to be able to convert your adviser equity to savings, the two basic options are 1) negotiate a success fee or 2) negotiate a revenue or profit share. For number 1, be crystal clear what the definition of *success* is and what the corresponding fee will be. "When your income reaches $500,000 for the year, write me a check for $50,000." Or "When we reach ten thousand members on our Web site, pay me $1,000." For number 2, base your revenue and profit share agreements on a calculated percentage, like "10 percent of net profit for three years" or "5 percent of everything we sell over $100,000." Make sure you have a clear exit and that both you and the company feel great and equitable about how finances will be handled for each foreseeable outcome.

2. NO PEEKING IN THE UNDERPANTS. When codeveloping adviser equity deals based on percentage, it can be really tempting to overcomplicate the deal to try to capture every possible ounce of value for every possible foreseeable outcome. We've seen too many proposals that start to read like the tax code: "If the new revenue is more than 13 percent greater than the previous quarter, not counting any business from customers listed in schedule A . . ." etc. Yuck! As an adviser, you end up having to audit their financials in order to be sure that you are being treated fairly, which can feel to the business owner like you're "peeking in their underpants." Also, the more complex the math, the more opportunity for multiple interpretations of reality. "You meant all revenue *after* we take out refunds, didn't you?" It's best to keep the deal dirt-simple. For this reason we'd even suggest you stay away from any *profit* participation and deal only in *revenue* sharing. Profit is open to interpretation and requires that you agree with how expenses are categorized. Revenue can often be determined just by glancing at the first line of a bank statement.

THE WEALTHY LIFESTYLE, BEFORE YOU HAVE THE WEALTH

When a typical investment fails, you lose. When an investment in adviser equity fails, most of the time you still win. *Informal* adviser equity is the same gratitude-based benefit that you get for helping people become successful with *formal* adviser equity, only without the formal contract. Sometimes it's not appropriate to ask for stock or success fees, but you still want to help. One such time is *after* a project that you've been helping with fails.

The gratitude that fuels adviser equity doesn't die with the company or project. It lives on in the heart of your mentee. If you both believed in a successful future at some point (even though you both turned out to be wrong), it's very likely that at some point in their career they are going to find themselves with more access to resources. At minimum, the goodwill you've created will create value for you in the form of enthusiastic introductions to people you want to meet.

Sometimes, your informal equity—earned either through reciprocity for the general attitude of generosity and contribution that you've developed or as a result of continuing a friendship after a failed formal equity agreement—can turn into very real financial returns. We've both received many gifts as signs of gratitude from those we've helped but had no formal agreements with, including all manner of vacation invitations, exclusive experiences we couldn't even pay for (such as invitations to very exclusive events, parties, and the kinds of experiences you'd associate with the lifestyles of the rich and famous), and access to all kinds of luxury experiences. Many of these gifts were given by people with access but without ownership: people who are influential but not necessarily wealthy. And many of them came to us from surprising places: people whose influence was not known to us when we were devoting a little bit of our time to helping them with their most important goals. We received these benefits in exchange for our own advice: all manner of informal relationship advice we've provided to people in difficult situations personally or professionally, career advice, mediation and conflict resolution, high-level problem solving, writing advice, making connections and introductions (especially helping the adolescent and twenty-something children of people in our network with introductions for first jobs, mentors, etc.), and finding good investors for start-ups and good start-ups for investors.

It's difficult (and a bit foolish) to quantify just how much time we invested in this kind of informal adviser equity to garner such returns, and what we might have earned if we had demanded cash instead, but it's definitely less than 0.1 percent of the "sticker price" of the gifts we got in return. That's not taking into account that most of the people we were helping had no way to pay us at the time, even if they'd wanted to.

We are both experienced *adviser equity* investors and we've invested mightily in our ability to help other people succeed. Our investment "portfolio" shows it. Most of the experiences that we've had that make us *feel* successful came as gifts, not as a result of spending huge chunks of our savings accounts on luxury items. But you don't have to be a professional at helping other people to participate in adviser equity. You just have to be generous with the wisdom you've learned from your life's experiences to those who have not yet learned those lessons.

If social evolution is measured by the degree to which the younger generations can outpace the older in capability, advantage, and advancement, then participating in adviser equity is the best way to participate in that evolution. The more people in society actively help the younger generation shortcut the lessons they learned the hard way, the faster the growth rate of the younger generation will be, capturing greater value and greater efficiencies and reaching their own potential with less time and fewer resources expended along the way. The more successful younger generations are, the more "excess" equity they will have to increase the quality of life of their elder mentors. We envision a future in which everyone participates in a continuously shifting multigenerational equity structure, where young people are able to defer the cost of mentorship and starting up a business, and older people are able to defer the financial benefit until the time they want benefit without contribution, or "retirement."

CHAPTER 8

TRIBE

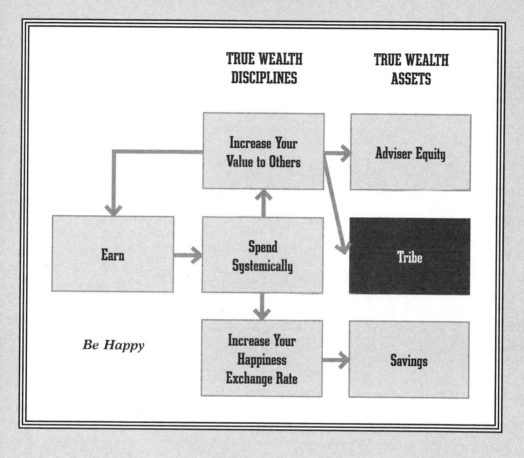

TRUE WEALTH DISCIPLINES

TRUE WEALTH ASSETS

Increase Your Value to Others

Adviser Equity

Earn

Spend Systemically

Tribe

Be Happy

Increase Your Happiness Exchange Rate

Savings

- THE VALUES OF A TRUE WEALTH TRIBE -

- CONTRIBUTION -

- FREEDOM -

- TRANSCENDENCE AND GROWTH -

- DEVOTION -

- COMMUNITY -

- TRIBE STARTING FOR THE UNINITIATED -

The ultimate True Wealth asset is coveted the least by those who have yet to obtain it, and—once obtained—is often sworn to be the most prized of all.

It was 2007, and Bryan was watching a pair of headlights approach in his rearview mirror. He had stopped short in the middle of the two-lane tunnel near his home in Alameda, California, to avoid the car in front. He had sighed in relief when his sports car's performance tires were able to grip the wet pavement well enough to avoid an accident in front. It had been a few seconds since the glare of headlights bouncing off the tunnel floor caught Bryan's eye in his rearview mirror, but the headlights didn't seem to be slowing down.

Bryan's last thought before the impact was, "Damn! I should be wearing my seat belt." Bryan's head injuries were pretty minor, though there were a few scary hours waiting for tests to come back in the emergency room to rule out internal bleeding. He learned one of the most valuable lessons of his life that day (in addition to the importance of wearing seat belts, of course). Sometimes life's most important lessons require a great deal of introspection to glean valuable insight from difficult experiences. By contrast, this particular lesson arrived quite plainly via text message. Actually, in a total of sixty-five text messages over the course of the next couple of hours.

A few months prior, he had fallen in with a community of people in San Francisco, many of whom lived together in a giant cohousing facility. It was an unusual experience for him, because before then, though Bryan had plenty of friends, for the most part they didn't know one another. Suddenly, most of the people he knew well *all knew one another.* And they didn't just know one another, but they all shared a deep and profound connection to one another—more loving and caring than some people have with lifelong friends.

Most of them talked about *the community* with such a sense of import and reverence that Bryan thought it odd. At the time, Bryan's associations with the word *community* were *community service* (basically punishment), *community center* (a place for poorly maintained pool tables), or *neighborhood community* (the people you live near but don't particularly like). He certainly enjoyed the range of interesting people in this *particular* community; there were artists, marketers, dancers, entrepreneurs, authors, activists, and even a couple of dot-com millionaires. But he didn't have any feelings at all for the idea of *community* itself.

Somehow, within hours of Bryan's emergency room visit, someone in the community had found out about the accident. Soon nearly everyone in the tribe had reached out to Bryan— even those he didn't know well yet. It was emotionally touching to know that that many people cared about his little mishap in the tunnel, but what was even more touching was the content of each of the sixty-five messages. They didn't simply say, "Dude I'm sorry you got in a car wreck I hope you're ok." They all contained some variation of this basic question:

"Is there anything at all you need?"

In the following weeks, even though Bryan made no requests for help, the tribe showed up with rides, meals, administrative help to handle the insurance companies, and a full complement of massage and physical therapy sessions to aid in recovery from whiplash and other minor injuries—all accompanied with the firm request that there be no financial remuneration of any kind.

The quality of care was so high and the purity of intent was so great that it took Bryan aback more than once.

"Why are you doing all this?" Bryan asked of one friend in the tribe.

"Because we're *tribe*," she said.

In this modern-day version of the ancient social structure, there is no official membership. There is no doctrine. There is no leader or chief. There are no rules. There's no secret handshake or initiation ritual. There's no being voted in or kicked out. There are implicit values, like *contribution* and *growth*. But there is no structure of enforcement or governance. Tribe is simply a networked group of friends bound by their caring for one another and for a similar aesthetic for life. But when a group of friends become networked—when each knows each other—something else, not available from a simple friendship, emerges.

That was the day Bryan first understood that the value of a tribelike community transcends the value of knowing its individual members. That the sum of this True Wealth asset is immeasurably greater than its parts. Even then, like a person sitting in front of an early personal computer, he had no idea of the full power of what he had discovered, nor had he the first inkling of how important it was going to be to his future.

———

There are, of course, great economic benefits to belonging to a tribe. Beyond saving a few thousand dollars on services relating to recovering from a fender bender, tribes introduce you to economic opportunity, new jobs, new customers, and new partners. Tribes save on expenses by sharing, and increase your Happiness Exchange Rate by providing people you love to hang out with. If we accounted for all of the potential economic benefits of tribe, it would probably qualify as a True Wealth asset on that basis alone.

But it would also be missing the point. Tribe is the only asset that acts *directly* on the purpose of your entire financial ecosystem itself.

The purpose of your financial ecosystem is for you to be happy, as in deeply satisfied with your life, and financially secure. Making money, saving money, and even the SAFE plan itself are all *strategies* toward that end. They are intermittent steps in order to achieve a specific endgame. But tribe isn't (just) a strategy. It contains the recipe for the endgame itself: satisfaction, happiness, and the experience of financial security. Tribe can "win the game" directly without the need for any strategies.

═══════════

Bryan and Jennifer, his business and life partner, were enjoying their yearly vacation on Tuesday of the Burning Man festival in 2011—sort of a "family reunion" for their tribe each year. Well, to be honest, they weren't really enjoying it. They had gotten themselves to a really difficult place in their relationship. Neither felt appreciated by the other, both were focused on what the other was doing wrong, and they were barely able to have a conversation that didn't end in raised voices or storming off into the dust.

They had been together for four years, they were engaged to be married, and *theoretically* each knew the other loved them. But they certainly weren't feeling it. This felt like a *serious* fight. In a peak of frustration, Jennifer removed her engagement ring. Though she later said it was just too painful to wear in that moment, and she wasn't giving up on the idea of being married, it scared Bryan into desperation.

He found two men in the tribe whose relationships he admires—we'll call them Andy and Allan—and asked if he could get some advice on how to unwind this downward spiral. What came next shocked Bryan, and became a turning point in his life as well as in his now-thriving relationship with Jennifer. It also cemented for Bryan the full understanding of the power of tribe.

Andy's idea was that he, his wife Ellen, Allan, his wife Natalie, and Bryan and Jennifer all spend the evening in an RV together and witness Bryan and Jennifer's conflict. Then, rather than Bryan and Jennifer trying to work it out, the other four would do the work of understanding the relationship dynamic and do their best to unwind it *for* them.

Bryan regards what happened in the next six hours as nothing short of a miracle. Every aspect of their unhealthy relationship pattern was analogous to patterns that at least one of the other couples experienced as well. But in the presence of two other couples who love not only Bryan and Jennifer, but their relationship as well, they were able to point out the blind spots one by one until both Bryan and Jennifer had entirely new perspectives.

Bryan and Jennifer left the RV arm in arm, feeling more in love than they ever had and, most important, coming to this life-altering realization: "As long as we have a tribe of people who love us and who also have the kinds of relationships we admire, we never have to suffer through another relationship issue alone." Since that day, we've found the same to be true in virtually all aspects of life, from money, business, and purpose to health, love, and sex—and we've found that to be a vital source of advice, compassion, and happiness.

THE VALUES OF A TRUE WEALTH TRIBE

Your tribe (whether you find it or create it) will be based on your aesthetic for life. If you like extreme experiences and high intensity, your tribe will have a very similar aesthetic. If you cherish silence and contemplation, you will find yourself in a tribe valuing the same. Membership in the tribe is based on sharing values—not on geography, social ties, economic status, achievements, or common interests. There are some key values that we believe are universally important for activating the self-amplifying nature of a network of close friends and utilizing the power of that network to enhance your True Wealth (and of course the True Wealth of your tribe-mates). Top tribe values should include:

CONTRIBUTION. This means giving what you can to advance the purpose and endeavors of other people in the tribe. The wins of others are naturally celebrated because it reflects positively on all the contributions.

FREEDOM. This means valuing a person's authentic self, authentic feelings, authentic expression, and authentic way of being *more* than any idea you have about how they *should* act, feel, express, or be. It's an invitation to find all the parts of yourself that you keep bottled up because you fear the disapproval of others and courageously share them with your tribe.

GROWTH OR TRANSCENDENCE. This means turning toward the mirror when you see something showing that you might be ashamed of. It means seeking feedback and valuing progress toward the higher stages and states of being that you and your tribe aspire to reach.

DEVOTION. This means valuing your commitments and your loved ones. It also means allowing yourself to be motivated by and devoted to something that you regard as larger than yourself.

COMMUNITY. This means valuing the tribe itself and actively stewarding your evolving understanding of the tribe's values and aesthetic. It means being more committed to the community than to any one person's membership.

People with a strong sense of community typically list their tribe as one of the top three positive influences on their happiness. How is it that a network of friends can be such a potent source of fulfillment, happiness, and security?

BEING, BECOMING, AND TRIBE

There are two sources of happiness or contentment that seem to be universal for all humans.

Being: Being means awareness of what *is*. An appreciation of the present reality—the underlying constant to the apparent changes of life. The feeling of belonging is an expression of being. When you look across the room into the eyes of your lover and say, "Wow! You are magnificent!" you are expressing a moment of happiness sourced in being. The part of us that wants to amass a huge savings account so that we don't have to work another day in our lives is, underneath it all, reaching toward a state of being. A state where nothing needs to be done, and all is perfect as it is. Being is the perfect expression of motherly love.

Becoming: Becoming means striving for what *could be*. It's why, deep down, you'll always want to be a better person, even after you realize that you are already flawless. It's what makes learning, development, and growth pleasurable—even without any secondary benefits. Becoming is the perfect expression of fatherly love.

Not enough being, and you experience burnout, self-judgment, workaholism, worry, and frustration. Not enough becoming and you get complacency, lack of engagement, self-delusion, laziness, apathy, and resignation. The right tribe can play the role of ideal parents acting like a 24/7 being/becoming gym, at once encouraging you to develop and further yourself and rewarding you for who you already are.

Most people value the experience of being "seen," "gotten," or "met" as among the most cherished experiences a person can have. Being seen usually means being accepted as you are, even in the face of exposing a part of you that you didn't think was worth accepting or that you didn't know you even had. Even the most gifted person delivering the experience of being seen can't give you as strong a dose as a healthy tribe that shares the above values.

It's normal for you to change your behavior slightly when you spend time with different people. If those friends don't know one another and routinely see you in the presence of one another, then each friend gets to see only one reflective facet of you.

But when your friends are networked, each sees a different facet and they compare notes. Your friends begin to see the composite, and each begins to relate to you as the whole you. Among a tribe that expresses the value of freedom and encourages you to bring your most authentic self (instead of your most successful self, or your most glamorous self, or your most funny or most any particular thing), you will find yourself able to completely relax. To drop your social expectations and pretenses. To find out who you are when you don't need to be any particular way. In short, to enjoy a profound experience of being.

Being seen can be a double-edged sword. When you are your authentic self, and you've removed the inner marketing department that constantly edits what you are doing and saying to gain approval from those around you, your tribe will also see your blind spots. Blind spots are psychological distortions that we apply to the world around us that we don't know we have.

Someone who is overly aggressive, but whose aggression is in his own blind spot, will project his own aggression onto the world and think that other people are either too sensitive or too quick to get angry. (Sensitivity and a quick temper are natural reactions to aggression.) A person who doesn't speak her mind enough, but whose silence is in her own blind spot, will similarly project her own hesitation to speak up onto the world around her (especially her romantic partner!) and believe that other people either don't listen very well, or are too silent themselves. If you carry a flamethrower around with you but you don't know it, you will live in a world where everything spontaneously erupts in flames all the time without any provocation. You might even find yourself saying, "Why are you always throwing fire at me!?" This is the mechanism by which humans blame others for their own affectations. These blind spots are often the biggest threats to your Happiness Exchange Rate, because they distort your view of the world (usually negatively) and kill the happiness you might have experienced otherwise. In fact, it's basically impossible to make a long-term positive change to your Happiness Exchange Rate without dealing with at least some of your blind spots. If you purchase a romantic outing for you and your sweetie but end up spending the evening fighting instead, you can be sure that blind spots—yours and your sweetie's—played a key role in how the evening turned out.

Usually, even *two* people can't distinguish blind spots effectively. If my blind spot is that I'm too aggressive, and your blind spot is that you don't speak your mind, how can we possibly sort out why you don't feel safe to speak up? In a binary system, one person's "convex" blind spot is the other's "concave" blind spot. Without at least a third perspective, you will never be able to be certain of what's actually real (which is why people can erroneously convince themselves that their life partner—though wonderful in many ways—is basically crazy).

But tribes can see these blind spots—and constructively point them out. Whether the context is romantic relationships, business strategies, parenting, learning professional skills, physical health, or creative expression, this natural blind-spot spotting creates an environment of constant development and growth. In short, a perpetual experience of becoming.

Tribes that are committed to contribution and growth are always searching for new ways to better themselves and be more in service to one another and the world. That means even a small tribe of twenty people can learn and experiment with twenty times as many new skills and approaches as any one member. When one person finds something that works, it tends to spread through the tribe like wildfire. In this way Bryan and Michael have witnessed waves of capability and accomplishment roll through their community of friends. Someone in the tribe discovers an excellent book on managing conflict in a romantic relationship, and not long after, *all* the romantic relationships in the tribe are functioning better. Someone discovers a more effective marketing technique for entrepreneurs, and a few months later *all* the entrepreneurs in the tribe have more effective marketing in their businesses. Dozens or even hundreds of people help one another maximize the benefit of everything they learn.

ECONOMICS OF BUILDING TRIBE

Like any system, tribes require more up-front investment than their single-unit counterparts (in this case friendships), but as they come online and self-amplification effects start to take place, the time and financial costs of meeting new people and maintaining old friendships are dramatically less. If you had roughly 150 friends, but no tribe, and you wanted to see them every other month, you'd have to have nearly 20 appointments every week just to maintain your friendships. Not feasible unless your only concern in life is to maintain your friendships. (Ill-advised local optimization!) But with tribe, you can easily maintain those same friendships by attending a single event, barbecue, or party every month or two. This raises your active network size from perhaps as many as a dozen well-maintained relationships to as many as 150.

Once your tribe has reached critical mass, the tribe itself is constantly attracting new people who share exactly the same values. In other words, the kind of people you most want to know socially and professionally will be busy finding you, dramatically reducing the need for active networking to maintain your entrepreneurial ecosystem.

But what about *before* your tribe has reached critical mass? How do you reach out into the social ether and start collecting the kinds of people you can build your tribe around?

Most people don't think of themselves as community leaders, or even *potential* community leaders. But we believe you are. What it takes to lead a community is an authentic commitment to the values of that community and the willingness to put in a little legwork to give the community opportunities to meet one another and form bonding friendships. When you do, you start to acquire what we call *connection capital*, utilizing the power of the convener, the power of social proof, and the power of positive associations, explained in chapter 3. Connection capital increases the number of financial opportunities (be they job opportunities or entrepreneurial business opportunities) and decreases the risk and cost associated with trying new things.

If you are still intimidated by investing in a tribe that could yield valuable connection capital, start with these tips:

NINE TIPS FOR THE UNINITIATED:
TRIBE STARTING AND CONNECTION CAPITAL

TIP 1: Choose a "Valuable" Value

We have lots of things that we value. We value art, music, relaxation, effective communication, healing, growth, community, leadership, contribution, great parties, funny jokes, and authenticity—just to name a few. Some of these things are more directly linked to our earning potential than others. Given that the nucleus of any tribe is its core values, and those core values will be the basis on which you attract new members, it is important to choose a set of values that are important to you, and that also relate directly to your earning potential. As a real example, building a tribe around the idea of investing in yourself, where each member is actively engaged in self-investment, is likely to yield more connection capital than investing in building a tribe around the core value of "getting wasted and fucking around," for example. If *Contribution, Freedom, Growth, Devotion,* and *Community* speak to you deeply as values, choose those.

TIP 2: Invite the Five or Ten Most Interesting People You Know, from Different Contexts

Think of five or ten of the most interesting people you know from different contexts—work, your fitness or yoga class, different social circles you're in. People who are interesting, and don't know one another. The common thread should be that they each represent an aspect of the core value you've chosen. If you choose based on value, like "self-investment," rather than context, like "people from the gym," then you are likely to get a diverse group that will mix well. Think about the most interesting people you know in each of these five main domains—the same domains we suggest balancing with your Systemic Spending:

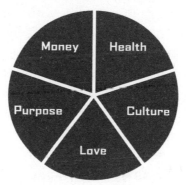

Eventually, your tribe should have each of these major areas covered by one or more people who achieve extraordinary results in that area—and do so relatively effortlessly. If you build a tribe full of creatives who are masters at culture but are unable to figure out how to pay rent each month, you won't be able to use the power of the tribe to transcend that set of issues or problems. Same if your tribe is deficient in people who have great love lives, healthy bodies, or a clear sense of purpose. Conversely, if at least some people in your tribe have created a powerful relationship to each area, then naturally, given enough time, *everyone* in the tribe will have a powerful relationship to *every* area.

The key is, there should be "diversity" to your interestingness. Just having rich people, or beautiful and fashionable people, or intelligent people, or geeky people, or whatever, is dull. (Have you ever been to a party full of rich bankers?) Aim to create a scene where guests are going to encounter a *diversity* of fascinating people. That is what will best build your connection capital, and that's how people get the most value out of your events. If a bunch of people who are exactly the same hang out, none of them learn anything new, none of them have their world expanded, and there will be no exchange of value.

Most people think that relationships are formed on the basis of what each person has in common with the other. We notice that stronger, more powerful relationships are often formed on the basis of what is *not* in common—provided that there is one recognizable core value that is emotionally important to each. This is another reason for coalescing around values. Values like "self-investment," "freedom," and "contribution" cross cultural and socioeconomic boundaries. A wealthy person with a challenged love life and an artist with health issues can find common ground in their values and build a strong bond, each helping the other in the ways most needed.

TIP 3: Ask Guests to Invite the Most Interesting Person They Know

We learned this concept from our friend Garrison Cohen, who used to host "Invite Your Most Interesting Friend" parties in San Francisco. If you have only five people coming, if you ask them each to invite an interesting friend, all of a sudden you can have ten to fifteen very easily. (Ten is a perfect number for an intimate dinner party.) If those ten to fifteen have a great time, you might have twenty-five to thirty RSVPs at the next event you host.

TIP 4: Host Events Regularly—Aim for Once a Month

Once you host your first event, and people have had the experience of meeting someone new and interesting at your event,
they will want to come back for more. Don't disappoint. The
key in building your connection capital is consistency. If you
host the next event in six months, people will forget about you
and you won't build connection capital. If you invite people to
the next event in a month, you'll start building momentum.
You'll also get better at it, and learn from experiences where
some guests might not have gelled as well as others, and you'll
start to develop ways to help people be more comfortable with
meeting new people.

TIP 5: Choose a Cool Venue

Nearly every bar and club in your city is looking to have more
people come in on weeknights, particularly between the hours of
five and nine p.m.—and also between those hours on weekends.
Dress nicely, walk into several classy bars or lounges in your
town, and ask to speak to the manager. Say, "I host networking
events where I get thirty to forty people together for connecting
over drinks. I'd like to host one of my events here. Is there a
space we could use on a weeknight from seven to nine p.m.?"

As an alternative, yoga studios and dance studios are every
city's greatest resource for underutilized event space. All across
cities in America, there are studios with space to fit hundreds
lying fallow on certain weekend nights. While some space owners understandably don't want any alcohol consumption on
their premises, other owners of these spaces are often thrilled

to find a way to make a few hundred extra dollars on a weekend night. Often, they can't sell drinks in their space, but you can rent the space for a flat fee and have your guests BYOB, or charge a small cover and give that to the space owner. The key with such spaces is to develop a relationship of trust over time, and to host only events there in which you know the guests will be respectful.

TIP 6: Keep the Invitations Peppy and Personal

The first impression that you make on someone new who comes to your party is not actually *at the party*. It's the invitation. You want it to be peppy and exciting. Most people, when they're throwing a party, basically just say, "Hey, I'm throwing a party on Friday. You should come, it will be awesome." That's a huge mistake.

When you ask someone to come to a party, you're asking them to invest hours of their time (the scarcest resource on the planet) and you're also asking them to choose your event above whatever other options might be available to them that night. You've got to give them a compelling reason why they should do so. That's why your invitation copy is so crucial. It needs to convey the benefits, and the excitement, of your event.

Here's an example of a successful invitation Michael wrote, which drew 150 people to a get-together he hosted in New York:

Summer Soiree in Red

You are cordially invited to pass a midsummer night in NYC at our Summer Soiree in Red.

We can't believe an entire season has passed since our last Soiree, in which 150 of you packed the place (and drank 150+ bottles of champagne—wow, go team!).

Mingle with all your friends, make new friends, forge ever new business connections, trade business cards if you have to, or better yet, stolen glances, or late-night hidden kisses on this sweltering midsummer night, shake yo' thang, and enjoy the company of people like you . . . who *like* you.

WEAR RED!

Please bring somethin' to drink for sharing, and/or snacks to share (fruit, cheese, chips, chocolate, cookies, etc.).

Friends are welcome, if you feel they are awesome and would fit in well with the group.

–>Attire: Sexy and RED!

Please RSVP to me so we can keep tabs on #s, and make sure any friends you invite RSVP too.

Love,

Michael

Spell out the benefits that people would get from attending the event—meeting new friends and the possibility of romance are ever-popular benefits. If you're hosting a strictly professional event, obviously, you should tone down the dating/romantic innuendo of the invitation, but no matter what, you should always focus on benefits in your invitation copy.

Also, notice how Michael talked (truthfully) about how successful the last event was. As in online social networking, in offline party hosting, the power of social proof ensures that nothing succeeds like success.

Keep your invitations personal. You want to invite people *from your own e-mail address.* It doesn't have to be your main personal e-mail address, but create one address, with your name in the "From" field, to invite people. This increases the sense of personal connection with your social scene.

As much as we love Facebook, we've found that the RSVP rate for events promoted through Facebook is extremely low. Using online invitation services like Evite or Punchbowl is better, but still not as good as plain old personal e-mail. We don't recommend using list management software like iContact or Constant Contact. That just adds one more layer of depersonalization. Remember, this is not a mass e-mail list like you might develop through an online opt-in form from a Web site. This is a list of friends and friends-of-friends you've cultivated through face-to-face connections at offline events. Keep the vibe as personal as you can.

To supercharge your RSVPs, send individual e-mails. This is the one single trick I've found that most up-levels the RSVP rate. E-mail invitations individually.

Simply write, for example:

> Hey John,
>
> It was great seeing you at the last event. [For extra brownie points, insert some personal touch if possible.] I was so happy to hear about your new job. How are things going with it?
>
> I'm hosting another event next Friday. I'd love to have you there! Details are below.
>
> Hope to see you soon!
>
> —Michael
>
> ———
>
> [Cut and paste the invitation copy here]

Doing this takes a lot of time, but it will typically double your RSVP rate. We think it's well worth it to make your events rock.

TIP 7: Treat Your E-mail List Like Gold

By now, you should be developing an e-mail list of people who have come to your events. If you keep encouraging people to bring their friends, you should be able to fill out thirty to forty people in a great venue with no problem. You may end up with two hundred to three hundred names on a list of people who have been to past events and who want to be notified each time you are doing something similar. This list is gold—almost literally—because of the monetary value that will likely come from opportunities sourced from this group over time.

Treating your list like gold means:

1.   Don't share it with anyone. Ever.

2.   BCC when sending a note to more than one person on the list. Just using "CC" is basically sharing someone's personal contact information without permission. Also, everyone will get a dozen replies when others hit "Reply All" in their RSVP. Yuck.

3.   Keep it safely in one clean place—like a spreadsheet on your hard drive. Back this up as this list is very valuable to you.

4.   Send people only what they want to know about, and give them plenty of opportunities to opt out. You can just include a reminder at the bottom that says, "If you'd no longer like to receive event invitations from me, just let me know and I'll take you off this list immediately."

TIP 8: Make Your Events Free, or as Low Cost as Possible

We do *not* recommend trying to make a business out of your event organizing. We know very few people who make good money selling entrance tickets to their own social events. And the strategy here is about building a tribe, a social scene, and *giving* to those people. If you really invest thought and care and effort (and some money) into the events you organize, the people who attend will be very grateful that you've given them this gift. You will be paid back indirectly through this gratitude in thousands of ways, large and small, that go far beyond money you get directly out of their wallets. Investing in building your tribe is Systemic Spending that is going to help you build an asset that will be a sustainable and repeatable source of financial opportunity and personal enjoyment.

TIP 9: **Invest in Your Ability to Connect and Do Business with Affluent People**

Choosing to connect *only* with wealthy people in your social and professional network is cheesy, but choosing to *ignore* wealth or success as a factor when deciding whom to connect with is equally ignorant. Learning how the wealthy are different and how to create the kinds of events they value could be one of the most financially important skills you learn.

There are two excellent books on this topic. First, we recommend *Networking with the Affluent* by Dr. Thomas J. Stanley. This book teaches you how to become a high-value adviser in helping powerful, connected, influential, and affluent people get what they want, thereby becoming invaluable to them. Stanley teaches you how to take on high-value roles in their lives such as "The Talent Scout," "The Advocate," "The Revenue Enhancer," "The Family Advisor," and "The Mentor." One of the easiest ways to become wealthy, powerful, and influential yourself is to become the person who helps wealthy, powerful, influential people.

Second, we recommend *No B.S. Marketing to the Affluent* by Dan Kennedy. In this book, Kennedy points out the danger of overrelying on middle-income customers as your sole source of revenue. In a down economy, middle-income customers button their wallets on all nonnecessary spending, vastly reducing their expenditures.

His main insight is that, for high-income clients, their main concerns are first, getting the result they seek effectively, and second, avoiding hassle and wasting time. If you can provide an offering that gets them the result they're looking for effectively, in a way that does not waste their time or cause them hassle, they care about price much less than other segments. Using this strategy, Michael doubled his copywriting rates overnight (and has doubled them again since then), seeking out a clientele who were shopping on quality rather than on price, and never looked back.

Wealth is not an indicator of a person's value, intelligence, impact, contribution to society, or even social status (particularly in communities that value nonmonetary wealth). Ensuring that you attract wealthy people doesn't mean that you are *giving up* on attracting your other values. It doesn't mean that you no longer care if they are interesting or if they represent the core value of your tribe. It means that it is worthwhile to understand the cultural differences that most often correlate with wealth, so that people who are interesting *and* represent your core value *and* have a lot of monetary resources are attracted to and enjoy participating in your social circle. The best tribes have people from a wide range of socioeconomic backgrounds. The more diversity, the more cross-pollination, the more integrated and well rounded each member of the tribe becomes.

At a certain point, and we trust you'll know it when it happens, your tribe will take on a life of its own. You won't be the one organizing all the events anymore, and you may find your tribe merging and growing with other already-existing tribes. Once your tribe has a life of its own, step back/down as its leader. If you are always *the* leader, people who like your values but don't necessarily want to be *led* by you will be repelled by your group. If you let tribe leadership go to your head and try to control who's in and who's out, pretty soon your tribe is going to look more like a cult or an entourage.

Don't measure the success of your tribe by the number of members, by the fame or success of the members, or even by your tribe's reputation. Measure your success by the degree to which your tribe provides deeply authentic *being* and *becoming* experiences, enhances the value of the True Wealth assets of everyone in the tribe, and by how well the tribe lives by its values.

How long are you welcome to stay as a guest in other people's homes? And in how many homes? This is a True Wealth measure of financial security. Knowing that you've built enough relationship capital to survive living the rest of your life even if your earnings or savings take a huge hit: that is a feeling of safety that even the worst credit crisis or global economic meltdown can't erode.

CHAPTER 9

THE FUTURE OF FINANCIAL SAFETY

"**F**uturism is no longer optional," says our friend the marketing and entrepreneurship trainer Eben Pagan. What he means is that there used to be a time when one could get along fine without thinking too much about the major trends sweeping through society; one could feel comfortable that there would always be safe jobs, government and corporate benefits aplenty, and lots of social safety nets for those who fall behind.

Obviously, that world no longer exists, and the changes sweeping through society are happening so swiftly that everyone must think long and hard about what the future holds. We can no longer count on government or corporations to think about future trends for us; we must think about these trends for ourselves, and plan accordingly.

This, in a sense, turns *everyone* into an investor, whether we like it or not. Investing can be thought of as a commitment of resources, in light of your best, informed guess as to what the future will hold (such as the future of stock markets and housing markets, as in the FACD plan, or the future of your earning power, as in the SAFE plan). In this sense, even choices such as where you live, what skills you invest in, and whom you know become investments.

OUR PREDICTION: A SHARING ECONOMY, WITH PRESTIGE BASED ON CONTRIBUTION

Everything we've written in the book so far has been based on direct experience. We've experienced the benefit of what we're advocating ourselves, seen others in our tribe benefit from it, or, usually, both. In what follows, we change perspective. We are now switching to speculating about the future. This is the version of the future we're betting on—not just with words, but with nearly every choice of how we spend our time and money.

═══════════

The dream of comfortable retirement in a single-generation, single-family home is dead. The run-up in home prices of the last fifty years (which funded the retirement of previous generations), the ballooning educational debt loads of people in their twenties, the stagnation of wages due to downsizing, outsourcing, and offshore competition, and the persistent inability to save mean that this prospect is unlikely for most young Americans.

Does this mean a bleak, dreary future for them?

Not necessarily.

Fortunately, young people today are pioneering the very tools, values, and practices that are going to save them: the sharing economy. They are doing this because it is "cool" and cheaper to move in this direction. But they don't realize that while they are building this cool, cheaper alternative, they are also building their own life raft.

The previous American Dream was based on ownership: earn and save enough to own your own home, your own full set of major and minor appliances, your own home entertainment setup, car(s), yard, tools—all for one family, at most. All of this ownership requires enormous cost, for purchase and maintenance, forcing young people to remain at hard work just to keep up. After researching this book, we now believe that this dream was intentionally sold to the American public starting in the 1940s to intentionally increase redundant spending and artificially drive up the GDP, and that the single family home was invented as a symbol of achievement to get America "back to work," even as it destroyed the multigenerational ties that had provided lifelong security since the invention of "retirement" a few hundred years prior.

───

It was an appealing dream for the privileged, and it's understandable why millions of people went for it. But, whether we think it's a nice dream or not, it's a dead dream. It is simply out of reach for most young people today, who wince at the pitiful starting salaries being offered to them in entry-level jobs, and who may not even pay off their student debt until their thirties.

So, today's young people are doing what young people always do: innovating with new ways of living. Do a Google search for "cohousing." (Add "start-up" or "entrepreneur" before that phrase to find the particular segment of the cohousing world we are talking about.) This is the beginning of a major trend we see sweeping through the nation in the coming decades. It is starting primarily in Silicon Valley and the Bay Area, which in multiple areas from technology to cultural, political, and sexual trends to gay rights has been a leading indicator for the nation.

Young people are finding that even the dream of *renting* their own apartment is out of reach now. So they have taken advantage of the fact that it's actually more *fun* to live in a community, not to mention much less expensive, if that community is well run and well functioning. There is now an explosion of cohousing homes, communities, corporate and legal structures, innovation, best practices, technology platforms, and, most important, values spreading throughout the Bay Area—and soon, we predict, throughout other urban areas, such as New York, where there is high demand for affordable yet livable housing options for young innovators.

This trend is based on young people capitalizing on a very basic insight: *using* an asset is almost as good as owning it (and often better, when used with your friends), at a fraction of the cost and maintenance. In the past, people have stayed away from the sharing of assets, because the logistical hassles and transaction costs in time and money to make the sharing work smoothly and fairly were prohibitive. Now, with Web sites devoted to allowing the sharing (or microrenting) of nearly any asset imaginable, from apartments to cars to bicycles to garden tools, there is much less need to buy any one of these things, while enjoying the benefit of all.

Another reason people have stayed away from the benefits of sharing has been that it seemed more prestigious to own things. Never underestimate the power of the drive for prestige. However, a new form of prestige is arising, in tandem with the sharing economy, which we believe is making this shift away from ownership, and toward sharing and community, inevitable.

PRESTIGE BASED ON EXCLUSION VS. PRESTIGE BASED ON INCLUSION

One reason many people view the coming trends toward sharing skeptically (instead of getting ahead of the curve, as we suggest) is that they have negative associations with the concept of sharing. "Share your toys with your brother/sister!" was never as fun or as affirming to hear as "This toy is all yours, and you decide who gets to play with it."

Any type of prestige based on excluding others, as in sole and private ownership, we call *exclusionary prestige*. While the drive for prestige has manifested in millions of unique expressions—as varied as the people who seek it—there are two broad categories of exclusionary prestige: mainstream and countercultural. Mainstream prestige is based on acquiring and owning the primary goods, accomplishments, and achievements promoted by the mainstream of any given culture. In American culture, this includes owning the biggest home possible, driving the most and best cars, having the best educational credentials possible, having the most power and status in one's job, marrying the most high-status mate (with status defined along traditional markers), and having children who go on to do all of the same. This form of prestige is exclusionary, because one person owning a home means someone else cannot own the same home, and so forth.

Running counter to this mainstream form of prestige has always been a variety of countercultural forms of exclusionary prestige. Today, these systems are embodied in the young person's cultural ideal of the hipster. The hipster may not have enough money to live in a nice apartment, but he knows the coolest bands, and if you don't know those bands, you're not cool enough for him. The hipster may not be able to afford high fashion, but she knows how to repurpose thrift-store clothes with just the right amount of irony, so that the irony itself becomes the prestige marker, not the clothing to which the irony is attached. The hipster may not have a law degree, but he can spout far-out postmodern philosophies of art and aesthetics in a manner that sounds just as impenetrable and exclusionary as the jargon of the mainstream masters of finance and law.

Amid this prestige battlefield emerges a new form of prestige— one that benefits the people who seek it, *and* everyone else as well. This is a prestige based not on how elite someone is, or how cool someone is, but on how much they *contribute.* Its most modern expression can be seen in Silicon Valley, with the advent of the open source movement. In open source communities, everyone can plainly see one another's contributions and judge for themselves the degree to which those contributions (usually in the form of technical solutions to shared problems) benefit the community. Those who contribute more become favored, even quasi-famous. This prestige, just like its exclusionary cousins, is so attractive that some of the most talented developers and engineers contributed millions of hours of their valuable time—without any hope of financial gain—just to get some of it. In the process, enormous projects like Wikipedia and the music genome project (the heart of music service Pandora) were built almost entirely on these volunteer efforts.

Prestige based on contribution can be thought of as *inclusionary*. It must include, not exclude, more and more people, because would-be contributors need "customers." They need people to contribute to.

With this contribution-based model of prestige spreading across the Internet in the last fifteen years, it is no surprise that it has begun to leap off the page, into the lives of the young people who are exploring it online. As these very same people work on open source projects during the day, they often do so in a shared cohousing home, in a shared living room, over shared Wi-Fi, grazing on meals and snacks that have been prepared according to a shared meal plan, listening to music over the shared stereo system.

You might assume that this sharing is all need based. Young people can't afford housing (true) so they have to settle for a lower standard of living by sharing (false). In fact, some of the wealthiest people we know—even those with a staggering nine-figure net worth—are living in these same shared homes.

A culture or society that wants to encourage people to share doesn't need to rely on socialist ideals of selfless sacrifice, the faltering point of so many communal societies in the sixties and seventies. Rather, it can depend on prestige—but inclusionary prestige, based on size and impact of contribution.

Inspired by the open source ideal, this shift is happening among the most entrepreneurial segments of today's young people. They are adopting a set of values that, we believe, are the best investment for the future, given what we see as obvious trends toward more communal and shared living among tribe.

These are the traits that will make you an invaluable member of a community and a tribe. They include:

- An orientation toward contributing to, and making the biggest impact possible on, the lives of those around you.

- An orientation toward "curating" the people you want to spend a long time with, so that your contributions to them feel like high-quality investments in your tribe, and therefore you want to make more and more of them.

- Accountability. Learning how to take feedback well, without getting defensive, and learning how to deliver feedback in a way that doesn't trigger other people's defensiveness.

- Empathy. Understanding why other people feel and think the things they do, even if you don't agree with them. This makes living together and sharing exponentially easier.

- Working on your "stuff." As described in chapter 8, we all have blind spots that massively disrupt our ability to live well with others if left unaddressed. Investing in therapy, coaches, and, most of all, face time with your community and beloveds is the best way to bring blind spots to the fore and address them.

- Developing a "clean" communication style. If you can't express your emotions, particularly anger, disappointment, jealousy, and sadness, without causing a tornado of drama around you, you're going to have difficulties finding people willing to share with you.

The modern world's sixty-five-year-old experiment with hyperindividualistic living is about to retire, bankrupt and poor in old age. If you're reading this, you don't need to suffer from the fate of this now-bankrupt form of investing. Do what all great investors have always done: figure out what the likely trends are, and align yourself with those trends. A tidal wave is about to rip through the American Dream and FACD-based retirement.

You can get crushed by this coming tidal wave. Or, as we

have consistently advocated throughout this book, you can SAFEly learn to surf.

TRUE WEALTH

Investopedia, one of the largest personal finance and investing sites on the Web, defines the discipline of economics as "a social science that studies how individuals, governments, firms and nations make choices on allocating scarce resources to satisfy their unlimited wants."[1] Another textbook tells us, "Individuals and businesses have unlimited wants and needs. However, the economic resources that can be used to meet their needs are limited. This mismatch of unlimited wants and needs and limited resources is known as *the basic economic problem*."[2]

If the basic economic problem facing humanity is how to satisfy infinite wants and needs with finite means, then we have a big problem indeed. After all, you *cannot* satisfy an infinite desire with a finite resource. You cannot even *sort of* satisfy an infinite desire with a finite resource. The mismatch is not one of degree; it is one of category. It's like saying that the fundamental economic problem facing society is how to build a house out of air. To build a house, you need things that build houses, such as hammers and nails. And to satisfy an infinite desire, you need things that satisfy infinite desires: namely, infinite resources.

How much love does a person want? Infinite love. Love is also, fortunately, an infinitely available resource.

How much self-acceptance does a person want? Infinite self-acceptance. Self-acceptance is also, fortunately, an infinitely available resource.

How much of a sense of belonging does a person want?

Infinite belonging. Belonging is also, fortunately, an infinitely available resource.

How much communion with a force greater than oneself (be it a spiritual force, a nation or community, an ideal, or existence itself) does a person want? Infinite communion. Communion is also, fortunately, an infinitely available resource.

Once a person is alive and minimally subsisting, his capacity to give and receive love, acceptance, respect, trust, belonging, wonder, and awe is infinite. We may rarely feel this sense of infinite capability; in fact, we're often quite aware of what we consider to be our limitations. What makes these resources infinite, however, is that whenever you have the experience of reaching your limit, there is always immediately more capacity to give and receive. There is, for example, no *inherent* limit on the capacity to give and receive love. Any resource for which this is true we call an "infinite resource."

If the basic economic problem is the mismatch between finite resources and infinite desires, then false wealth is the *accumulation* of finite resources in the hope of satisfying infinite desires. We call it false not out of some moral condemnation, but because it doesn't even make logical sense; the ends are not related to the means. It's like trying to score a goal in soccer with an interpretive dance, or to bowl a strike with a poem.

As opposed to false wealth, one way to think of True Wealth is a person's:

- Capacity to satisfy infinite values with infinite resources.
- Capacity to satisfy finite values with sufficient resources.
- Self-awareness to know the difference.

One of two false beliefs tends to prevent people from accumulating True Wealth. First, some people, seeking more happiness, love, or other existential or spiritual rewards in life, take refuge in platitudes such as "money can't buy you love," "money doesn't buy you happiness," or "the best things in life are free." They interpret these to mean that they can live a richly rewarding life without ever acquiring the capacity of satisfying their finite needs. This life path always leads to a continual struggle to make ends meet, which—ironically—impairs their capacity to receive, give, and savor the very love and happiness (and other infinite values) they thought they'd be able to get for free.

The inverse tragedy occurs for those who believe they can indeed satisfy infinite values with finite resources, if they just accumulate enough of them. Infinite values like happiness and fulfillment in life often hold out the illusion of being just around the corner. One more promotion at work, one more decimal place in the bank account, one more luxury watch, one more pair of shoes, one more dress size, one more "hit," and I'll be happy. Even though moments of attainment in the past have only ever provided a very short sense of fulfillment and satisfaction, it can be utterly convincing that next time will be different. This life path leads to the need to take more and more extreme measures just to maintain a baseline of happiness—sometimes culminating in addiction, mental health crises, extreme burnout, and bitter divorces. The emotional toll of these circumstances is often so great that, ironically, it also interrupts a person's capacity to meet his basic financial needs.

Avoiding either the former or the latter pitfall requires the self-awareness and maturity to distinguish between your finite and infinite values, and enact a life strategy that values the capacity for satisfying *both* categories.

Food, electronic gadgets, sex, exercise, and home theater systems are examples of what we call "finite values." There is a point at which you have enough food. And a point (which many Americans reach every single day) at which you have *too much* food. The same can be said for any finite desire, want, or value.

When economists suggest that you have infinite desires, they didn't imagine you eating infinite food, or losing infinite dress sizes. In other words, they aren't suggesting that your desire for any single thing is infinite. Rather, they suggest that, as soon as your desire for one thing is satisfied, you'll still want an infinite number of other things.

Yet, think of any moral, spiritual, political, or artistic hero you admire, from the past or present. Very likely, at a certain point their life stopped being defined by the chase for ever more variety and quantity of finite values. Rather, the desire for finite value *itself* was substantially satiated. Their life came to be defined by the cultivation of one or several infinite values, which they were able to embody and spread beyond any limitation of finite resources.

We have consistently observed, in others and in our own lives, that successful cultivation of core infinite values, over time, creates a threshold of general life satisfaction after which there's no sense of scarcity of finite value. At that point, the entire "economic problem" as defined by an endless rat race to satisfy ever-expanding needs comes to feel absurd.

It is the attempt to satisfy infinite values—love, wonder, awe, belonging, and the universal ideals of truth, beauty, and goodness—with *finite* resources such as money and material items that gets us into trouble.

In this book, we aim to help you invest in your capacity to tap into the infinite resources within you, and within the people around you, so that you can finally begin to satisfy your infinite desires, which have remained so chronically unsatisfied via attempts to accumulate false wealth.

At the same time, we have aimed to help you invest in your

capacity to generate finite resources, so that you can satisfy all the finite values you want and need, in *sufficient degree*.

What is "sufficient degree"? Only you can answer that. But we can tell you this: your answer will be more accurate the more self-awareness you have. And the more accurate your answer, the fewer financial resources you'll waste in misguided attempts to satisfy infinite values with the finite resources of false wealth.

Learn to satisfy your limited wants with limited means, but do not give in to the folly of attempting to satisfy infinite wants with finite means, as the definition of economics recommends. Infinite wants can only be satisfied with infinite means. These, taken together with your finite means and your self-awareness, are the heart of True Wealth.

Our greatest hope for you is that you use the two capacities of True Wealth—tapping into infinite values, and generating finite ones in sufficient degree—in combination, to live an extraordinary life. A life defined less and less by working hard to earn money to consume things that you thought (incorrectly) would buy you happiness. A life more and more guided by the realization of your highest ideals.

ACKNOWLEDGMENTS

FROM BRYAN

I am fortunate to be thoroughly bonded and partnered with my wife, Jennifer Russell, so deeply that every thought that swims through my brain is built on some foundational belief or idea that we forged together. As a result I could easily footnote her for every line written in this book. I credit countless hours of ideation and debate with Jennifer for any aspect of the thinking represented in this book that you find to be intuitively wise, holistic, or profound.

Throughout the process of writing this book, my coauthor Michael has taught me enough about writing to, well, fill a book. But more than that he taught me how to *be* a writer, to adopt the identity of a writer, to organize my thoughts as a writer. This book represents my proudest professional accomplishment to date, and it simply wouldn't have been possible without the generous invitation and loving collaboration provided by Michael. The depth of his generosity and finesse of his guidance cannot be overstated.

My parents, Lee and Marijo Franklin, gave me not only life, but also the frameworks for exploring and understanding it. Each a pioneer in the area of business leadership, they passed on their wisdom and experience to me in an extraordinarily artful way of parenting that left me feeling fully loved and accepted as I am while simultaneously reinforcing my evolutionary desire to become more. Thank you, Mom and Dad.

Thank you to the strategic geniuses whom I've been fortunate enough to coach and mentor, including especially executives and CEOs Paul Sutter, Reid Hoffman, and Richard Greene. And thank you to the hundreds of guides, gurus, leaders, peers, and mentors who have influenced my thinking so much over the years and dedicated their lives to the same bright future we all see is possible—especially Eben Pagan, Jay Abraham, Annie Lalla, Nathan Otto, Nathan Patmor, LiYana Silver, Darryl Anka, Sheridan Brice, and Daniel Schmachtenberger.

FROM MICHAEL

At the early stages of my own writing on this book, before I brought Bryan on board as my coauthor, I needed a lot of support conceptualizing it. I was extremely lucky to have Sandor Gardos, Michael Vassar, and Sarah Constantin as frequent interlocutors, idea bouncers, reality checkers, and general ideation muses. These brilliant people, whom I am lucky to call friends, all made themselves available to me for long hours, often on short notice and through the middle of the night. I am extremely grateful to all three of you for your support of this book; thank you so much.

The book also benefited from my discussions about it with Peter Shallard and Jena la Flamme, and early interviews with Victor Cheng, James Altucher, Ramit Sethi, and David Heinemeier Hansson.

Jena la Flamme was extremely patient and encouraging with me as I worked long hours on the early drafts; thank you, soul-sister, for your support, always.

Thank you to my agent, Esther Newberg, for arranging us another wonderful opportunity to work with Portfolio; we couldn't have been happier with the placement. And thanks again to Sandi Mendelson for connecting me to Esther.

Adrian Zackheim at Portfolio, as always, provided extremely valuable big-picture guidance on the direction of the book. Maria Gagliano offered wonderful editorial advice on earlier drafts, as did Matthew Hutson. Niki Papadopoulos came in on later drafts to make it tight as could be. Thank you all.

Bryan, you are a dream to work with. This was my first true collaboration ever; thank you for teaching me how. Every bit of this book reflects your wisdom and brilliance.

Much of this book was written, on my side, while listening to my musical muse, Adey, whose masterpiece albums *Rogue* and *Vesica* I come back to again and again when I need to be reminded what it's all about. Thank you for lighting my ears—and all that is between them—dear Adey: your art is my great teacher about True Wealth.

Thank you, Daniel and Patricia Ellsberg, for giving me all.

NOTES

Hyperlinks to Web articles can be accessed at
http://www.ellsberg.com/last-safe-investment-notes.

Introduction

1. "Compound Annual Growth Rate (Annualized Return)," Moneychimp, accessed August 30, 2015, http://www.money chimp.com/features/market_cagr.htm; "S&P/Case-Shiller U.S. National Home Price Index," S&P Dow Jones Indices, accessed August 30, 2015, http://us.spindices.com/indices/real-estate/sp-case -shiller-us-national-home-price-index.
2. Donghoon Lee, "Household Debt and Credit: Student Debt," Federal Reserve Bank of New York, February 28, 2013, http://www.new yorkfed.org/newsevents/mediaadvisory/2013/Lee022813.pdf; Meta Brown, Andrew Haughwout, Donghoon Lee, Maricar Mabutas, and Wilbert van der Klaauw, "Grading Student Loans," Liberty Street Economics (blog), Federal Reserve Bank of New York, March 05, 2012, http://libertystreeteconomics.newyorkfed.org/2012/03 /grading-student-loans.html.
3. Joseph E. Stiglitz, "Student Debt and the Crushing of the American Dream," *The New York Times*, May 12, 2013, http:// opinionator.blogs.nytimes.com/2013/05/12/student-debt-and-the -crushing-of-the-american-dream/.
4. Aleks Krotoski, "Robin Dunbar: we can only ever have 150 friends at most . . ." *The Guardian*, March 13, 2010, http://www.theguardian .com/technology/2010/mar/14/my-bright-idea-robin-dunbar.

Chapter 1: Investing to Increase Your Happiness Exchange Rate

1. Paul Byrne and Simon Boyle, "Revealed: The big-spending businessman who ran up a £203,948 bar bill was a 23-year-old

City whizkid," *Daily Mirror*, March 06, 2012, http://www.mirror
.co.uk/news/uk-news/the-businessman-who-ran-up-203-752576;
"Currency Converter," Oanda, accessed August 30, 2015, http://
www.oanda.com/currency/converter/.

2. Harry Bradford, "Alex Hope, 23-Year-Old Millionaire, Arrested
   in UK for Trading Scheme," *The Huffington Post*, April 04, 2012,
   http://www.huffingtonpost.com/2012/04/04/alex-hope-arrested
   _n_1385392.html.

3. Michael Ellsberg, "John Mackey, Co-CEO of Whole Foods, and
   Marc Gafni on 'The Unique Self of Business,'" *Forbes*, January
   12, 2014, http://www.forbes.com/sites/michaelellsberg/2014/01
   /12/john-mackey-marc-gafni/.

Chapter 2: The Super Skills

1. "Leading CEOs: A Statistical Snapshot of S&P 500 Leaders,"
   Spencer Stuart, September 2006, http://content.spencerstuart
   .com/sswebsite/pdf/lib/2005_CEO_Study_JS.pdf.

Chapter 4: Invest in Creative Super Skills

1. "Blindman No. 2," *The Blind Man*, (May 1917), http://sdrc.lib
   .uiowa.edu/dada/blindman/2/05.htm.

2. "Duchamp's urinal tops art survey," BBC News, December 1,
   2004, http://news.bbc.co.uk/2/hi/entertainment/4059997.stm.

3. "The loo that shook the world: Duchamp, Man Ray, Picabi," *The
   Independent*, February 20, 2008, http://www.independent.co.uk
   /arts-entertainment/art/features/the-loo-that-shook-the-world
   -duchamp-man-ray-picabi-784384.html.

4. "Piero Manzoni," Conceptual Art Debate, accessed August 30,
   2015, http://conceptualartdebate.wikispaces.com/Piero+Manzoni;
   "Currency Converter," Oanda, accessed August 30, 2015, http://
   www.oanda.com/currency/converter/.

5. "Merde d'artiste: not exactly what it says on the tin," *The
   Guardian*, June 13, 2007, http://www.guardian.co.uk
   /artanddesign/2007/jun/13/art.

6. "Dada artist accused of vandalizing Duchamp piece," *USA
   Today*, January 06, 2006, http://usatoday30.usatoday.com/news
   /offbeat/2006-01-06-duchampfountain_x.htm.

7. Daniel Pink, *A Whole New Mind: Why Right-Brainers Will Rule the Future* (New York: Riverhead Books, 2005).

8. Seth Godin, "Creativity and stretching the sweatshirt," Seth Godin (blog), January 27, 2009, http://sethgodin.typepad.com /seths_blog/2009/01/creativity-and-stretching-the-sweatshirt .html.

9. "Business Buzzwords Generator," *The Wall Street Journal*, accessed August 30, 2015, http://projects.wsj.com/buzzwords2014.

10. Ronald Alsop, "M.B.A. Recruiters' No. 1 Pet Peeve: Poor Writing and Speaking Skills," *The Wall Street Journal*, January 18, 2006, http://www.wsj.com/articles/SB11374391058 9047733.

11. Richard A. Lanham, *Revising Prose*, 5th ed. (White Plains, NY: Pearson Longman, 2007).

12. Charlie Munger, *Poor Charlie's Almanack: The Wit and Wisdom of Charles T. Munger*, 3rd ed. (Virginia Beach, VA: Donning Company Publishers, 2005).

13. Brook Thomas, "The Education of an American Classic: The Survival of Failure," in *New Essays on the Education of Henry Adams*, ed. John Carlos Rowe (Cambridge, UK: Cambridge University Press, 1996), 26.

14. "The Hero with a Thousand Faces," Wikipedia, accessed August 24, 2015, https://en.wikipedia.org/wiki/The_Hero_with_a _Thousand_Faces.

Chapter 6: Invest in Physical Super Skills

1. Michael Pollan, *In Defense of Food: An Eater's Manifesto* (New York: Penguin, 2008).

2. Kai Ryssdal, "How many work emails do you get a day?" Marketplace, July 9, 2012, http://www.marketplace.org/topics /life/final-note/how-many-work-emails-do-you-get-day.

3. Sue Shellenbarger, "On the Job, Beauty Is More than Skin-Deep," *The Wall Street Journal*, October 27, 2011, http://www.wsj .com/articles/SB10001424052970203687504576655331141 820484.

4. Megan Willett, "12 Scientifically Proven Ways to Make Yourself More Attractive to the Opposite Sex," Business Insider, August 14, 2013, http://www.businessinsider.com/how-to-attract-the -opposite-sex-2013-7.

Chapter 7: Adviser Equity

1. Joshua Prager, "Secretaries get rich in the Internet age," ZDNet, April 21, 1999, http://www.zdnet.com/article/secretaries-get-rich-in-the-internet-age/.
2. "Charlie Ayers," Wikipedia, accessed August 30, 2015, http://en.wikipedia.org/wiki/Charlie_Ayers.
3. Nathan Olivarez-Giles, "Google's first hire, Craig Silverstein, leaves for start-up," *Los Angeles Times*, February 9, 2012, http://articles.latimes.com/2012/feb/09/business/la-fi-tn-google-first-employee-craig-silverstein-leaves-for-education-startup-20120209.
4. Nick Bilton, "Facebook Graffiti Artist Could Be Worth $500 Million," *The New York Times*, February 12, 2012, http://bits.blogs.nytimes.com/2012/02/07/facebook-graffiti-artist-could-be-worth-500-million/.
5. "Seagate Number of Employees," Macroaxis, accessed August 30, 2015, http://www.macroaxis.com/invest/ratio/STX--Number-of-Employees.
6. "A Brief Overview of Employee Ownership in the U.S.," National Center for Employee Ownership, accessed August 30, 2015, https://www.nceo.org/articles/employee-ownership-esop-united-states.
7. "Frequently Asked Questions," SBA Office of Advocacy, accessed August 30, 2105, http://www.sba.gov/sites/default/files/FAQ_Sept_2012.pdf.
8. Meir Statman, "How Many Stocks Make a Diversified Portfolio?" *Journal of Financial and Quantitative Analysis 22*, no. 3, September (1987).

Chapter 9: The Future of Financial Safety

1. "Economics," Investopedia, accessed August 30, 2015, http://www.investopedia.com/terms/e/economics.asp.
2. Les Dlabay, James L. Burrow, and Brad Kleindl, *Principles of Business*, 8th ed. (Mason, OH: Cengage Learning, 2012), 12.

INDEX